The Dating Booklet

Practical Guidelines For Life-Giving Relationships

Martin Connor, LC

ISBN: 978-1-716-01337-9

Interior design by Booknook.biz

"It seems that we can never give up longing and wishing while we are alive. There are certain things we feel to be beautiful and good, and we must hunger for them."

George Eliot

CONTENTS

Acknowledgments

THE TEAM OF COLLABORATORS FOR this booklet offer our deepest gratitude to the many others who supported this work by reading, editing, and offering feedback from personal experience. In particular, we would like to mention the following: Michael and Kelli Byrnes and family, Camilla Tirado, Grace and Molly Wills, Blaise Connor, Peter Devine, Kyle Marchuk, Alexandra Cathey, Tom Curry, Brittany Garcia, Mary Henkel, Deidre Merrill, Le Doan, Jimmy Mitchell, Fr William Brock LC, Arden Coakley Buchanan, Cecilia Pappas, Pat and Sarah Tramonte, Sean and Christina Delaney, Chas and Katie Ratliff, Jamie Riley, Rudy Martin, Patrick and Michael Agrippina, Fr Juan Pablo Duran LC, Sofia Hernandez, Josie Hartney, Austin and Olivia Leslie, Christina Yao, Fr John Klein LC, Jake and Sarah Martin, Fr Anthony Sortino LC, Ana Gutowski, Patrick and Margaret Hanus, Vince Frese, Sean and Christina Delaney, MacKenzie Eden, Madeline Zuniga, Julie Voss, Gabe Virnig, Jude LeCompte, Sean Delaney, Ben Volandt, Adam de Olano, Brittany Morales, and Louis Ho.

Special thanks: Maria Hernandez for drawings; Joann O'Neil for editing.

Cover design by Ana Gutowski.

Introduction

FULFILLING RELATIONSHIPS: WHO DOES NOT WANT SUCH RELATIONSHIPS IN THEIR LIFE?

1. It is love and love alone that brings fulfillment. Yet most of the time today what we hear and see regarding love is not love. It is about "use." We *use* things, we *use* objects. People are neither. We are persons. Persons were meant to love and be loved. Most don't understand what love really is and they don't know the distinction between love and use, but they are aware of the feeling of being used. Being used by another (and not loved) hurts a lot.

This booklet is making the serious assumption that our reader is desiring a love that is authentic, pure, real, and at times very sacrificial. It is an expression of a total gift of self to another person without any "payback." It is *this* love that is the bedrock of any fulfilling relationship: be it family, friends, or marriage. It is *this* love that calls us to look for what is best in and for the other. It does *not* look for what appears to be best for ourselves. *This* is the meaning of the word love when used in this booklet. It is *this* love that is like a little flame that is gradually nurtured with small acts of love (kindling), igniting love to grow ever stronger. Dating nurtures this love between two persons who are looking for a mature love, a blazing fire.

Hence, when you read the phrase "***this love***" throughout the booklet, you know exactly what we are speaking about.

2. Dating is the social interaction whereby men and women should actively seek out a relationship based on *this love*, and, ultimately, get married or else move on. If you understand dating as something else, like hanging out with friends, having fun, enjoying romantic attachments, or as a means to satisfy a sexual need, then this booklet will invite you to open your mind and challenge your perspective. We need to celebrate the good in relationships and, at the same time, point to the integrity and vitality of love as essential to long-term happiness. Maturity and readiness for marriage should be considerations in the decision to date.

3. This booklet advocates dating with this spirit of intentionality. Take the word courtship, for example, a word commonly used less than 50 years ago but now seemingly archaic. Important decisions concerning justice take place in a court of law. Courtship implies the same – its purpose is to come to a decision about a commitment to marriage. The philosophy of ethics says something similar: every conscious choice takes one either closer to or further from the desired end. The BIG picture, the final end is heaven, but there are also a lot of little "ends" that move us in that direction. Following this logic, every date should help one move in the direction of a decision for marriage.

This dating booklet is designed to offer guidance to people about what they must do to worthily engage in relationships of *this love*. Based on the human desire to love and to be loved, the booklet offers an honest pathway of both self-assessment and couple assessment which is ultimately meant to help explore the possibilities leading to marriage or to part ways.

4. The daily choice of *this love* is challenging. The truth is that we have a lot of choice in who we aspire to be as individuals and choice in the people with whom we fall in love. The best place to start is to ask ourselves if we are currently making good choices that could attract the kind of person we would want to love.

Such self-assessment can help all our relationships flourish, particularly ***that most important relationship*** we hope will lead to a lifelong commitment in marriage. In a long-term commitment like marriage, this same love is elevated to a unique plane by a physical relationship. Two people cling to each other as both a gift and a need. It is a profound human act that represents both a deeply felt need and entails a free gift of self. They become literally one flesh and one life through the gift of children.

FIVE IMPORTANT BUILDING BLOCKS FOR THE DATING ASSESSMENT

1. **Dating is important yet demands maturity.** Dating is a healthy activity that helps one grow and learn about oneself and about other people. Yet, it does have its risks that demand a level of maturity. Due to its often emotionally charged nature, dating works best between two responsible adults. This does not mean teenagers shouldn't date, but their level of maturity is important. Responsible, mature people shoulder their part of the dating relationship, but they don't put up with harmful or inappropriate behavior.

2. **Dating is about respecting the value of every human being.** This attitude warns us of a selfish dating spirit prevalent in today's society. The objectification of others is one of the principal causes of pain and loneliness in our world today. We have inherent dignity as *persons*; we are not *things*. From this inherent truth about ourselves, potential relationships and healthy partnerships can grow.

3. **Dating is for assessing.** It is not for "playing." We are dealing with other human beings who deserve the best of us, not the worst. In other words, all the stages of dating are serious because you risk causing the other person harm. This is why dating requires an ongoing mature evaluation of yourself and the relationship. It is not meant to be an unhealthy cycle of constant questioning, but rather a series of steps to bring you and the other person to a

more mature and responsible place in life. Ultimately, this process should help you discover whether you are either meant for each other or if it is better for you to part ways, wishing the other every blessing.

4. **Dating requires good choices which come from personal introspection.** Good choices honor the other person and strengthen mutual respect. Yet, they tend to be more consistent when one makes time to ask him or herself: How am *I* doing? How are *we* doing? Deeper level thinking, facilitated by real "down time," is a rare commodity today in our frantically busy world. Nevertheless, this is exactly what we need when we are trying to figure out what we are actually seeking in our relationships. The alternative is simply to stumble through dating hoping "that it will all work out in the end" and not really having any clue what that may look like. You are encouraged to take time to reflect. Perhaps you can journal as you go through this booklet so that you may better understand yourself and your relationship and hence commit to *this love*.

5. **Dating based on authentic human love can be defined as a triangle with 3 very human sides: passion, intimacy, and commitment.** "The biological side of the triangle is *passion*, the spine-tingling sensation that moves us toward romance. The emotional side of love's triangle is *intimacy*. Love without intimacy is only a hormonal illusion. The cognitive and willful side of the love triangle is *commitment*. Commitment looks toward a future that

cannot be seen and promises to be there until death."[1] Ultimately *this love* seeks the good of the other person and involves all three sides, though one side may predominate over the others at different times in the relationship.

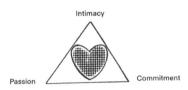

This dating booklet hopes to encourage growth in mature love. Chapter One will center you on the continual need for personal self-growth and the key factors needed to arrive there. More than "fixing" the "other person," we need to first understand ourselves. This is a lifelong task, worthy of attention both before and after marriage. Chapter Two will guide you to understand where our Creator and his master plan fits into the aspirations you have for love and marriage. The phenomena of attraction between people is the subject of Chapter Three. Chapter Four addresses the common fears that can debilitate you in your relationships. Honoring the good of the other by setting boundaries is discussed in Chapter Five, while living in the often negative "reality" of a virtual world is covered in Chapter Six. The first stages of healthy dating are outlined in Chapter Seven, and the last stages of healthy dating ending with engagement are in Chapter Eight. Living together before marriage and the common issues surrounding

---

[1] Les and Leslie Parrott, *Saving Your Marriage Before It Starts* (Grand Rapids, MI: Zondervan, 2015), 43-45.

that decision are explored in Chapter Nine. The final chapter offers recommended resources for your continual growth and enrichment.

Paula, 27 years old, single, medical professional

"It is good to be intentional about dating and seeking out that "right" person, but joy is important at every stage of our life. It is not worth being disappointed or feeling alone if dating or marriage does not happen when I expect it to happen. I must compare my life to no one else's, and realize the experiences and opportunities given to me in this stage of my life are incredible, beautiful, and uniquely timed gifts. They are experiences that should fill me with gratitude. If I use this time wisely, it will be a blessing and truly help me grow in ways I never imagined."

CHAPTER 1

Personal Growth

1. Fruitful and fulfilling relationships require a commitment to self-growth which consists in striving for excellence in the areas of our life that count the most, such as character development. We are all capable of growing in character and taking responsibility for our own actions.[2] Yet, *this love* is less about me and more about others, because it challenges me to give the best of myself for the good of others.

---

[2] "Good character is that quality which makes one dependable whether being watched or not, which makes one truthful when it is to one's advantage to be a little less than truthful, which makes one courageous when faced with great obstacles, which endows one with the firmness of wise self-discipline" (Arthur Adams).

2. If dating is about love, then in order to date someone, you must be a loving person. The following reflection really nails this: "Love happens because you are giving love freely in many different ways. Start with little things—like allowing yourself to appreciate a beautiful sunset or music or art. Search your environment for people to love. Make new friends and find ways to contribute to their lives. Volunteer for a cause that allows you to give your time and energy to people in need. Gradually, these heart-opening experiences will make you more receptive to love and you will naturally attract someone with whom you can fall in love."[3]

3. We need to be responsible for our choices in life and not shift blame onto others in an attempt to preserve our egos out of selfishness. We are called to be the best version of ourselves and must be willing to do our part in love. That means recognizing our shortcomings and seeking to overcome them in order to give ourselves in a more selfless way. If we can learn to love better, we can achieve true, lasting happiness, because, ultimately, love is central to human happiness.

Happiness in a relationship is less a mystery than it is a mastery of certain skills.

[3] BelovedHeart, "How Do You Define 'Falling in Love'," *Beloved Heart Musings and Journal* (blog), December 29, 2009, https://belovedheart.wordpress.com/2009/12/29/how-do-you-define-falling-in-love.

4. Self-growth is a path that avoids an attitude of, "they are the problem." It is motivated by the conviction that we are not born with the habits and skills that make our relationships flourish. We need to work hard on developing these habits and developing these skills to begin working on this fundamental attitude of self-growth. Every relationship, from family to friends to romance, demands it.

FIVE KEY IDEAS THAT HELP ACHIEVE SELF-GROWTH AND FUEL HEALTHY RELATIONSHIPS

1. Self-Possession: Putting Your "Own House" in Order

❑ It is important to know the state of our own house. That's where self-possession comes in. Self-possession includes self-knowledge, self-acceptance, and self-improvement. Regarding self-possession, the dictionary defines it as the state or feeling of being calm, composed, and confident. Personal growth begins with self-possession: putting our own house in order before venturing outside. In order to give ourselves to another in love, we must first master ourselves and then we will ultimately find ourselves.[4]

❑ Self-possession implies two things: (1) personal ownership and (2) responsibility towards the other. Personal ownership speaks to having greater control of our

---

[4] Karol Wojtyla, *Love and Responsibility*, (San Francisco: Ignatius Press, 1993), 98.

drives, passions, and motivations; it requires a true self awareness of the good and bad. It avoids the extremes. Responsibility towards the other, rather, seeks the good of the other. *This love,* expressed through self-possession, is **not** a *what's in it for me* approach; it is a pure love.

❑ Self-possession empowers one to use their human and sexual powers intelligently in the expression of love as self-gift: a *whole* person freely giving themselves to another, both body *and* soul, in marriage. Self-possession should be the truest and best expression of who we are as human beings.

Jamie, 22 years old, single, nursing student

"When I practice selfless acts for others, then I will be able to bring more of an abundance of love and fruitfulness to my own relationships. Practicing this early will encourage and shape a healthy lifestyle. It will pave the way for greatness with my own self-possession, for my future marriage, and for my life."

2. False Self-Possession: A House Made of Cards

❑ A house made of cards collapses. If self-possession is key to laying a strong foundation of love, then the opposite, a counterfeit self-possession, is a weak foundation.

We live in a culture where people often don't care about others and where the dignity of God's creation is of no importance. False self-possession is an expression of this indifference. It is not knowing your dignity. The "disposable" culture has had its influence on the dignity of human love. The objectification of self or another person, as just one more *thing* to use and discard, carries with it terrible consequences: depression, suicide, violence, substance abuse, and much more.[5]

❏ "We cannot treat ourselves or others disrespectfully and think it will not affect other areas of our *persona*. Consider, for example, a common belief today about our bodies. One hears things like 'my body is mine' and 'I can do whatever I want with it,' as if the body is separate from the rest of 'me.' It is a common view to treat the body like any other material object to be owned, controlled, or possessed. Experience shows we cannot disconnect our core selves from our bodies. This is a false self-possession."[6]

❏ The truth is: my body *is* me! How I treat my body is how I ultimately treat myself, because we are one and the same! Body, mind, spirit, emotions: "All of

---

[5] Bob Laird, "Uncoupling the Hookup Culture," *Los Angeles Times*, May 28, 2013, http://articles.latimes.com/2013/may/28/opinion/la-oe-laird-hookup-culture-20130528.

[6] Martin Connor LC, *Reclaiming Love*, (Washington DC: RC Spirituality, 2020), 14.

me" is good. If we choose to expose our bodies and souls to harmful experiences, then there will be painful consequences affecting "all of me." Our essence, as human persons, is an integrated unity of body and spirit. We are good because we have dignity as persons and not as things. Since we are body/soul composites, what we do with our body will impact our soul. A life of treating our body carelessly will negatively affect our entire persona. Each of us desires to be respected and honored — not to be objectified and used. We see this misuse so often today, resulting in pain and loneliness.

☐ Self-possession leads to *this love* because it involves getting the whole person, body and soul, to work together. It is a challenging pathway that attempts to free us from selfish attitudes towards other people. It requires maturity, a lived experience, and a continual free choice of restraining "my selfish side."

This love is intentional, and it takes practice. Such intentional practice is freely chosen and will affect all of your relationships from family to friends to dating.

Sean, 25 years old, dating, Advertising

"Be mindful of your intentions. A simple exercise I ask myself is 'why am I entering this relationship?' It is very okay not to have a great idea at first, however when you meet someone, very quickly feelings and impulses overcome reason. In order to protect yourself and your potential partner's heart, you need to always keep this in mind. 'Am I on stable ground for this relationship?'"

---

3. Choosing Freedom to Love Well

❑ In light of self-growth, it is critical to understand the true meaning of the word "freedom." *This love* must be free. Freedom consists not in doing what we like, but in having the right to do what we ought. Is not the best use of our freedom to love another person?

❑ Our development as persons depends strictly on the way we use our freedom, and we are all responsible for our own development as persons. We need to own the process. Our misuse of our freedom has consequences—sometimes tragic ones. We like our freedom, yet we do not always grasp the seriousness of the *responsibility* that comes with it. "The built-in reluctance to accept responsibility is so much a part of our fallible human nature. It is not surprising to find it at work in regard to our most fundamental task in life: determining what sort of person we shall be."[7] We are all tempted to deflect our responsibility elsewhere and blame our failures on factors over which we have no

---

[7] Germain Grisez and Russell Shaw, *Beyond the New Morality* (Notre Dame, IN: Notre Dame Press, 1980),159.

control, like our heredity and environment. No doubt there are life issues that impact us. They can limit our freedom, but not completely. Instead of lamenting over our situation, the challenge is to identify those factors that are actually within our control. What are we doing with the freedom that we *do* have?

❑ A free human being is precisely that person who makes choices that will lead them to be the best version of themselves. The "Golden Rule" (Mark 12:31), treating others as you would like to be treated, is *the best choice.* The bottom line is that love makes us better human beings. The misuse of freedom, by contrast, gradually allows outside forces to dictate our choices and behavior, quite often to selfish ends, and inevitably leads to a state of self-inhibiting slavery.

❑ If our love is somehow inhibited or even enslaved by something, then it is not *this love* — whether we are aware of it or not. A host of disordered desires and other selfish tendencies can enslave our love. For example, the physical attraction to another person overcomes our decision to remain faithful to a committed relationship. Other examples of this can include binging on TV, video games, shopping, or alcohol. When the attractions of lesser goods enslave us, we are not free to choose the best good for us. This leads to a life of turmoil and chaos.

The mere ability to freely choose something that is not good for us, or even evil, "because we can" is not a "superior" freedom. Rather, it is a liability of human freedom.

What do we mean by this?

☐ A "free person" is not someone who rules others. A free person is someone who rules themselves. They take responsibility for their actions. For example, an alcoholic is not free when he or she has an equal 'chance' to drink or to abstain. They are truly free when they can regularly choose sobriety. A free person makes choices that help them acquire the skills and aptitudes necessary for self-governance. These include courage, justice, resolution, collaboration, hope, and self-control. We do not arrive at this "freedom" without a lot of personal effort and help from God and others.

Louis, 33, dating, Analytics Consultant

"We do not applaud someone for just being able to choose. We applaud them when they choose the right thing, when their choice is virtuous and for the good of others."

Faith Community

4. Family, Friends, and Community as a Training Ground for Love

❑ Family or community life serves as a system of forces that form the person we are becoming. It is like a training ground for love. If we tend to be selfish and unforgiving with others, such as our family, then such habits appear in all our relationships. When the standards of the "Golden Rule" are affirmed in the family consistently over time, they communicate "*this is a good thing to do, this is how you treat another person,*" and they become a habit. The healthy and consistent giving and receiving of love in family and friendship is the critical training ground for forming the habit of *this love.*[8]

❑ Life-giving relationships need to be intentionally sought. Start now by seeking out deep relationships over superficial ones. They will help you continue to forge the right habits of *this love* in your life. Specifically, we need to be *around people who inspire us with the way they live*. Their example, particularly in how they love, will motivate us to strive for the same ideals, which will move us to choose the same path. True friends, for example, desire the best for the other. Friends should

---

[8] Mayo Clinic Staff, "Friendships: Enrich Your Life and Improve Your Health," *Mayo Clinic* (blog), August 24, 2019, https://www.mayoclinic.org/healthy-lifestyle/adult-health/in-depth/friendships/art-20044860.

hold each other to higher standards and expect to call each other out when they fall short. It's not something we like, but it's something we know we need. Not just anyone should have access to your personal life. Unfortunately, today, many people "over share" their personal life (to anyone and everyone) on social media. Be intentional to avoid doing this. Save the sharing of your personal life for only trusted, time-tested friends.

❑ For those who may have come from broken homes, or might not have those "good" friends, all is not lost. *Foundational relationships* that help transform us are always possible in life. First, make sure you assess your own situation in an honest way. The human person is frail and broken. Some past experiences demand professional attention like counseling or therapy. In whatever form that may take, mistakes and wounds from our past can have an impact on our identity, self-worth, and relationships with others and with God. Professional help provides us with tools to use to work through and undo the knots in our hearts that developed from bad choices or experiences.

❑ Finally, a community of people who support you, particularly a community of faith,[9] is also vital to dating. This topic is undervalued and even ignored by

---

[9] The first Christians relied on their community of faith, and we should, too! (Acts 2:42-44).

many young people. The unseen benefits of linking your dating life to a community of faith are many. Yet, all the benefits flow from one simple principle: We are educated in *this love* through *witnessing and participating in* healthy life-giving relationships. Faith-centered people strive (however imperfectly!) to believe in a good beyond themselves, a transcendent good, and in that belief, they find a lot of motivation for *this love*. If you can unite yourselves around a common goal, higher than yourselves, you'll be looking outward to achieving that goal instead of only looking "inwards." Relationships that tend to look only "inward" often breed insecurity and criticism of the other. Being limited and imperfect, human beings will never be able to fully satisfy each other. Our world is bigger than ourselves.

Sean, 25, dating seriously, Marketing

"I think that having a close community of people is essential for any successful romantic relationship. Family and friends love you. That is why you trust them with your deepest problems and seek advice and guidance. When it comes to your relationships, only you have full autonomy to decide to stay or leave. This being said, if all of your friends and family have the privilege of getting to know this person, and there are a lot of concerns, then we need to take it seriously. They know me sometimes better than I know myself."

---

5. The Digital Mask

❏ Too much reliance on digital communication can hinder our self-growth. With today's technology we have never been more "connected," yet never more alone. Slowly but surely, we are losing the capacity to interact with living human beings face-to-face. It seems that such intense exposure to all sorts of media platforms can make us more averse to direct conversation. With social media, when online, one does not necessarily have to think or care about the person they are talking to, while in person, you are aware of their presence because you are looking at and listening to them. We can also hide behind a form of online perfectionism. It can *mask* our true selves.

❑ Unfortunately, this digital development does not change the fact that dating is fundamentally about *self-revelation*. Consider the fact that "asking someone in person to go on a date, or even calling the person and making your intentions known, requires self-revelation manifested in some kind of bodily form presented to the other — eye contact, pounding heart, spoken voice, nervous behavior, sweat, etc. Texting and 'swiping right' hide or eliminate most of this self-revelation."[10] The real, genuine presence of another person deepens who we are. To avoid this *very* human reality is only to fuel that which makes us *less* human: self-indulgence, small-mindedness, and cowardice.

---

[10] Terrence P. Ehrman CSC, *Man of God* (El Cajon, CA: Catholic Answers Press, 2017), 147.

HOW DO I KNOW I AM READY TO DATE?

Five Intentional Goals to Establish: A Pre-Dating Quiz

1. Life is a journey, and it is all about "baby steps" in self growth. How can we give ourselves to someone else if we lack self-awareness? We often jump into dating when we are not necessarily ready for it. Perhaps we might feel pressured to date or "be in a relationship." It's not enough to date for appearances. We can never achieve perfection, but based on the principle of human maturity, there are intentional goals that should be established in your life before you initiate a dating relationship.

2. What follows is a quiz about self-growth based on six behaviors known to be good, intentional goals. The ratings will measure a certain level of self-growth both externally and internally in your life. They are also key indicators for the human groundwork in building a relationship with another person. When you rate yourself, recognize the internal vs external behavior. Spend more time reflecting on the internal behaviors even though they may not be so "quantifiable."

3. Remember, we are often our own worst judges, so it is a good idea to also get a trusted friend to rate you on these points. The more objectivity one invites into this self-examen, the better. Complete the self-exam at the same time as your trusted friend but do not immediately show each other the final tally. Once both parties are finished, you may compare the final tally of your tests. The trusted friend should help keep you honest. If the final number tallied for all the points is under 80, then there is work to do before dating.

4. You will rate yourself on each point on a scale of 1 to 5 described as follows:
- 1 = I am very poor with this behavior.
- 2 = I am inconsistent with this behavior.
- 3 = I exhibit this behavior half of the time.
- 4 = I am fairly consistent with this behavior.
- 5 = This behavior is a habit in my life.

Self-Growth Quiz

I. Daily Commitments
- ☐ Forming positive daily habits is important to me.
- ☐ I keep proper hygiene.
- ☐ Physical health: I maintain healthy eating habits and exercise regularly.

☐ Spiritual health: I feed my soul with silence and reflection.

II. Dependability
☐ I can keep my promises.
☐ People can confide in me.
☐ I capable of going beyond what is expected of me, that is, I am not "all bark and no bite."
☐ I am usually punctual.

III. Authenticity
☐ I can be myself no matter who I am with.
☐ I take ownership of my mistakes.
☐ I am steadfast in holding to my values.
☐ I am true to myself when no one is looking.

IV. Self-Motivation
☐ When I commit myself to something, I can follow through.
☐ I consistently strive to better myself.
☐ I take initiative and try new things.
☐ I regularly seek to go beyond my comfort zone.

V. Emotional Awareness
☐ I think I know how to process my emotions.
☐ I have a positive opinion about my emotional life.
☐ I do not fall into the negative habit of either repressing my emotions or letting them control me.
☐ I am willing to talk about my emotions with others.

VI. Sacrifice

☐ I can forgo "my ways" for someone else's.

☐ I recognize that authentic love often requires sacrifice.

☐ I can love someone who I do not necessarily like. In other words, I can submit my more "intense emotions" to my good judgment when it comes to the good of others.

☐ I am willing to let go of bad habits/behaviors in my life.

	TOTAL

5. If you feel overwhelmed while reading this list of good behaviors, ***remember they are just targets***. No matter how attracted you are to another person, if you do not have some of the "basics" in place in your own life, how can you really get involved with another person? It is not really fair to them. Let's be clear that the journey of self-growth is lifelong. However, certain principles are key building blocks that are wise to have in place before initiating a relationship.

6. This self-examination is meant to help you be present *to yourself* so that one can then be present *to that someone else*. The question, "Are you ready to date?" is answered with, "Are you ready to marry?". One is ready to date when one understands that the goal of dating is to find the person they are to marry. The habits above are key indicators that one has the maturity to get serious about this chapter of his or her life.

> **Denzel Washington, Actor, Director, Producer, offers challenging words about hard work and commitment.**
>
> "Without commitment, you'll never start, but more importantly, without consistency, you'll never finish. It's not easy. If it were easy there'd be no Kerry Washington, no Russell Hornsby, if it were easy there'd be no Denzel Washington. So, keep working, keep striving, never give up, fall down seven times, get up eight. Ease is a greater threat to progress than hardship."

Prayer for Peace

Wherever we are in life and in our relationships, we need to try to live it out in peace. Prayer helps us find peace. This particular prayer from the great St. Anthony helps discover the peace God desires for us.

Be Satisfied with Me

Everyone longs to give themselves completely to someone,
To have a deep soul relationship with another,
To be loved thoroughly and exclusively.
But to a Christian, God says, "No, not until you are satisfied,
Fulfilled and content with being loved by Me alone,
With giving yourself totally and unreservedly to Me.
With having an intensely personal and unique relationship
with Me alone.
Discovering that only in Me is your satisfaction to be found,
Will you be capable of the perfect human relationship
That I have planned for you.
You will never be united to another

Until you are united with Me.
Exclusive of anyone or anything else.
Exclusive of any other desires or longings.
I want you to stop planning, to stop wishing, and allow Me to give you
The most thrilling plan existing . . . one you cannot imagine.
I want you to have the best. Please allow Me to bring it to you.
You just keep watching Me, expecting the greatest things.
Keep experiencing the satisfaction that I am.
Keep listening and learning the things that I tell you.
Just wait, that's all. Don't be anxious, don't worry,
Don't look around at things others have gotten
Or that I have given them
Don't look around at the things you think you want,
Just keep looking off and away up to Me,
Or you'll miss what I want to show you.
And then, when you're ready, I'll surprise you with a love
Far more wonderful than you could dream of.
You see, until you are ready, and until the one I have for you is ready,
I am working even at this moment
To have both of you ready at the same time.
Until you are both satisfied exclusively with Me
And the life I prepared for you,
You won't be able to experience the love that exemplified your relationship with Me.
And this is perfect love."

St. Anthony of Padua

CHAPTER 2

"In the Beginning" – Our Human Destiny is Love

1. From the beginning, human beings were different from the rest of creatures in the world. Despite living in a society that insists we are not different from animals, human experience and common sense tell us otherwise. We have a higher purpose. Two thousand years of Christian civilization have taught us that "man is a person, man and woman equally so, since both were created in the image and likeness of the personal God."[11] Our dignity flows from our ability to behave *in the image of God* (Gen 1: 26 *NRSV*) and this image is love.

---

[11] *Catechism of the Catholic Church* (New York: Doubleday, 1995), 2334.

God created us to love. We know this intuitively about love by the way we react with disappointment when we or others fall short in our ability to love fully. Instinctively we know we are called to be more. Our happiness is intimately linked to love. Love is where our special dignity and higher purpose is found. It is the fundamental and innate calling of every human being.

2. Human love is about a relationship between persons. We are relational because our Creator is relational. Through Jesus, one God as three persons is revealed to us. The Father, the Son, and the Holy Spirit are an intimate loving relationship of three persons. This is the mystery of God's inner life. By analogy, through marriage, man and woman are called to an intimate loving relationship. Man and woman are created to enter into a communion of self-giving, one to another, and their love may become fruitful in children[12].

3. A faith-based understanding of the human person takes its starting point in this Divine mystery of the Creator. God Himself is a relationship of love and calls each of us as His creatures to the same — an inner calling to be a gift

---

[12] "*May* become fruitful" is important to underline. Children are a blessing from God and not a "right" that couples have. Fertility issues do not spell a lack of fruitfulness of love. Openness and joy are the hallmarks of fruitful love.

to the other.[13] Taking this further, this *invisible* mystery of God's inner life as a relationship has become *visible* in the physical human world for us to see, concretely, through the human body.

It is as if God were saying, "If you really want to know me, then look at my human creation: the physical design of male and female. Both are made in my image and express characteristics of me." The giving and receiving language of love as self-gift is imprinted into the very biology of male and female. Human sexuality is much more than just physical acts but communicates this great mystery: **our deepest reason for being human, for even existing, is to be a gift to another**. Love as a total gift of self is truly our higher purpose. The very physicality of our human make-up is a manifestation of this.

4. This human capacity to share our very selves pervades our whole life and is not limited to bodily organs or genital activity.[14] In other words, everything regarding love is not just about the act of sex. One can love another person in a non-physical way, without any intention of physical intimacy. This becomes very important when you begin dating because marriage is a lot more than just physical compatibility. It is about *human* compatibility.

---

[13] St John Paul II's great insight was that the human body speaks a language of *gift*. The body and soul must coincide in their expression for a person to have integrity. The body must speak a language of truth and love.

[14] Mary Prokes, *Toward a Theology of the Body* (New York, T&T Clark Ltd.,1996), 95-96.

LOVE AND HUMAN WEAKNESS

The world is often about self-getting, not self-giving. Do I get good feelings? Am I looking to be fulfilled in some way in my relationship? Instead, it should be, I discover myself by making myself a sincere gift to others. How can I meet this other person's needs and love them more? ***To will the good of another*** - that is what sincere love is. Yet, when we try to love another person, it is not always easy or trouble-free. It seems to cost us effort – at times a lot of effort. In fact, the human person is not always lovable. Few things appear to be "true" today for everyone. However, human frailty *is* true for all. Every human person is weak and imperfect and therefore our loving is very imperfect.

HOW DID WE END UP LIKE THIS?

1. Those who profess a faith in God know the diagnosis. For at least three millennia, the Jewish tradition, followed by the Christian tradition, referred to this human experience as *iniquity* or the consequences of sin. It speaks of the rupture that took place between our first parents and their Creator, God. This rupture also fractured the harmony and wholeness within the human person causing inner rebellion. It is like our operating system is damaged. The light of reason is darkened, our will and its capacity to choose the good is weakened, and the world of our emotions has gone silly. A common concern in dating is to "beware of damaged goods." This is true for all of us

because, in a sense, we are all "damaged goods": Rather than *whole* human beings, we are broken and fragmented.

2. This interior fracture causes us to treat a person as a means to an end. It is ultimately a spirit of utilitarianism. This spirit can be expressed in many ways: What do I get out of this relationship? or What benefit or pleasure can I get from this? This type of thinking is indicative of "a love that uses." It can also bring about blindness. Self-deception is a terrible partner in love. Today's generation demands authenticity and views dishonesty as repulsive. If we desire to remain in the truth in the face of personal weakness, we have to be careful about lying to ourselves. We need to take a hard and honest look at any selfish tendencies.

3. Faced with our own weaknesses, our consolation is in the hope that God will never abandon us. We have the very power of God on our side to help us! Our whole selves – emotions, senses, reason, will, and body – all of us, matters to God, and in turn, should matter to us as well. God sends us redeeming grace to help us choose Him. Grace is God's life-giving water for the human spirit. It brings "light" to our reason, "strength" to our will, and "order" to our emotions. All of us have been redeemed! And this reordering helps us make good choices and, therefore, enjoy a happier life.

4. "Irresistible grace" does not exist. In other words, we have to freely desire to choose it. God is a gentleman and will

never force Himself on us; we just need to turn to him in humility and confidence. Grace empowers us *to say no* to the many negative forces and selfish tendencies that inhibit our relationships and say *yes* to the many positive choices that enrich and strengthen our relationships. When we say yes, the very power of God will begin to act within us and illuminate our thoughts, words, and deeds in ever-new ways. These positive choices in turn produce a good for oneself and for the other.

5. Nevertheless, progress in leaving our "old ways" and growing in *this love* is slow and arduous. With any relationship, especially in the long-term, there will always be times of suffering and sacrifice. Expecting and embracing sacrifice when it comes your way is an essential key to any fruitful relationship, romantic or otherwise, because it is living ***in the reality*** of human imperfection. The "yes" to love is a source of pain and suffering, because love always requires letting go of the "selfish me," allowing myself to be pruned and wounded. Love cannot exist without this painful renunciation of myself.[15] This principle holds true in every state of life. It is not easy, but it is so worth it.

---

[15] Connor LC, *Reclaiming Love*, 52.

CHAPTER 3

Love and the Phenomenon of Attraction

1. As we have seen, love is the most important human experience. We need love in our lives. We need to both give and receive love. In fact, God made us that way. Yet, we do not need just *any* love. We desire the kind of love that is *life-giving*, that is, centered on mutual respect. *This love* is a true valuing of the other person *as a person,* and not for what they can give me. *This love* is a gift of self to the other. This is love.

2. The truth of *this love* is ever more critical once you enter into the stage of attraction, which is the front door of all dating. We can be strongly attracted to the "vibe" of another person. It could be the physical attributes—body and good looks—or it could be the psychological attributes—masculinity or femininity. This involves an emotional attraction to the mystery of womanhood or manhood. Yet,

attraction-love is not a helpful guide in seeing the truth of the other. Our emotions can falsify attraction, perceiving a value that might not even be present. Once the natural emotional reaction towards those qualities dies away, often we are left disappointed, deprived of the good we thought we had found.

3. Both men and women can fall victim to idealizing the other or what could be called "false coloring." Nowhere else can this be seen to happen so clearly than with sexual intimacy. Biology shows us that when you are attracted to another person, your brain releases dopamine, your serotonin levels increase, and oxytocin is produced.[16] This causes you to feel a surge of positive emotion. Oxytocin is a hormone that acts as a chemical messenger, is released during sexual activity, and is linked to the intensity of orgasms. When people hug, kiss, or engage in sexual intercourse, oxytocin levels increase. It gives you the feeling of euphoria. Although oxytocin can enhance bonding, it can also encourage favoritism and prejudice. **Oxytocin can blind you to the truth of your relationship and the way you perceive your partner.**

4. Human beings are more than just animals that have basic attractions and instincts for food or sex. We are capable of self-determination and good will. We have the power to

---

[16] Healthline Parenthood, "Why is Oxytocin Known as the 'Love Hormone? and 11 Other FAQs'," August 30, 2018, https://www.healthline.com/health/love-hormone#dopamine-and-serotonin.

reason, to see the truth, and then direct our will to go after that truth. We do not have to be slaves to our emotions and passionate desires. We have two choices regarding what we do with that strong emotional attraction: see the other as a person like ourselves and as someone to respect and value or as someone we use and exploit as a means to achieve our own ends. We are more than our instincts! Attraction is the first and essential stage of love but needs to grow and mature into *this love* that goes beyond the mere physical or psychological attraction. Our higher purpose as human beings is to love and love well!

5. We often hear that a woman is attracted to masculinity (strength) and man to femininity (beauty). These are qualities of the person – but they are *not* the person. These qualities do not define us. A woman's value or dignity, for example, is not defined by how "pretty" she is. These physical qualities simply add to the person. The problem comes when strong attraction focuses on just these qualities and the pleasure we derive from them, instead of the value of the whole person. The attraction can blind us to the deeper, more important truth that should drive our thinking and acting: this is another human being here before me and not some "play thing." However, the message we so often hear is that we have no choice in the matter – we have to follow our passions and instincts. "It's only natural".

6. Yet, we are better than this! *This love* challenges us to put the other person first before our own immediate desires and *we can* choose this freely. Yes, this comes at a price. It challenges us and may cause us to pull back. "We are free to turn down the challenges of love, but we will find true freedom *only* in accepting them."[17]

7. The glue of a healthy relationship is not *just* the physical compatibility, but all of the elements of true life-giving *human compatibility or communion*. We could name this bonding or closeness or intimacy, but it is critical to our happiness. This plays out clearly in a long-term relationship, like marriage, when multiple levels of intimacy are required for unity of purpose, such as raising children; and perseverance in difficult moments. True self-giving intimacy (vs. self-getting) builds *communion* at all levels of the person: spiritual, emotional, physical, intellectual, and social.

THE CRISIS OF NATURAL ATTRACTION

1. Our modern, hyper-sexualized culture has warped the different forms of natural attraction toward the good of the other sex (male or female) into something merely erotic, and even inherently bad. Yes, the physical is included but it is not exclusive. God wanted us to see the good in "this guy" or "that girl" that we are attracted to—but beyond the merely physical. Both men and women naturally

---

[17] Jason Evert, *Pure Manhood* (Scottsdale, AZ: Totus Tuus Press, 2108), 38.

esteem and aspire to imitate the attractive qualities of both sexes: sense of humor, kindness, empathy.

2. However, our society has taken what is natural and healthy and twisted it. Seemingly every attraction between two persons has been reduced to a purely *sexual attraction.* Sadly, this has had a tremendously negative effect on good, healthy, same-sex friendships – crucial to healthy relationship development.

3. To say (as we are told) that your attractions define you is both dangerous and scary. I am attracted to a lot of things, some good and some quite bad, but they *do not* define my identity. Our identity is rooted in the fact that we were created in the image and likeness of a loving and merciful God. This is our true identity. We are sons or daughters of a good Father, and from this flows our sacred dignity as human persons.

4. Yet, the twisting goes further when human identity is reduced to mere sexual orientation. Hence the barrage of new, far-too-narrow labels like gay, straight, trans, etc. These labels do not include "all of me": the whole self, body *and* soul. *This love* is willing the good of the other and should never be reduced to merely erotic attraction.

5. True love involves a deep awareness of the dignity of our *wholeness*, our complete self-worth, body and soul. Our identity goes well beyond the physical. Genuine love

communicates more than just something bodily; it is the giving of my whole self to another *for the other*. In short, we need to avoid reducing *this love* to something less than it is.

Robert Barron, Priest, Author, Theologian, "Bishop of Social Media"

"You want to destroy yourself? Cling to your warring emotions; they will devour you. You want to save yourself? Hook those passions onto the infinite purposes of God and you will find yourself elevated, transfigured, enlightened. Pressed in the direction of sanctity, you will save your life."

THE DISTORTION OF HUMAN SEXUALITY

1. Our deepest reason for being human, for even existing, is to be a gift to another. Love as a total gift of self (self-gift) is truly our higher purpose. Even our male to female body-person experience speaks of being a gift to the other: the man giving all that he is as a gift to the woman and the woman opening herself to receive the gift of the man. It is not one-sided. It is mutual. Our bodies were designed to say this to one another. Yes, the sexual act speaks a language of *totality*. And this act actually reflects who God is: the source and essence of complete and total love.

2. Yet today, so often sexual intimacy is distorted and sadly reduced to something less than it is. It has become merely recreational. "Let's go the movies, Let's go for ice cream, Let's have sex." Our human sexuality is so much more. God meant the sexual act to be highly pleasurable and incredibly bonding, but it is also meant to be life-giving: babies! Sex is God's "design system" for filling the world with human beings so He can share life with us (leading ultimately to eternal life). This sharing of life is called the family. "The family is the place where every human being appears in his or her uniqueness and unrepeatability."[18] It is also absolutely necessary and it's the primary building block of any healthy society.

3. Families come into the world through sex, and family life is about love. It is also the primary way we are educated in giving ourselves in love. "Sex doesn't just say, 'I take you a little while' or 'I like your body.' Sex says, 'I give myself to you forever, and I unite myself to you. I want to join with you and with God in creating, raising, and educating children. Sex speaks the language of marriage.'"[19]

4. Human sexuality is ultimately the power of sharing oneself. It is human and not identical to the animalistic drive found in subhuman species. This human capacity to share our very selves pervades our whole life and is not

---

[18] Karol Wojtyla, *Love and Responsibility*, 305 (footnote no. 57).

[19] Marybeth Bonacci, *Real Love* (San Francisco: Ignatius Press, 1996), 34.

limited to bodily organs or genital activity. The fact is that we express our sexual identity in the way we walk, talk, dress, work, and recreate. Both man and woman are wholly sexual: body, mind, and spirit.

THE FACTS ON CONTRACEPTION

1. Given the recreational perception of sex, we see how contraception has become a very normalized part of relationships. When you separate babies from bonding, you are going to have problems. Let's start with the physical. Taking birth control pills is the most popular way to prevent pregnancy and seems to have become a daily routine for plenty of women. Yet the negative side effects of the pill are often ignored or minimized. Different forms of contraception come with different negative side effects, particularly the hormonal types. Here are a few of the side effects that can appear when using forms of contraception: Bleeding, bloating and nausea, high blood pressure, depression, moodiness, loss of libido, sore breasts, cancer risks, headaches, appetite and weight fluctuation, vaginal

irritation, blood clotting, etc.[20]

2. After reading this litany of possible side effects, why would anyone want to expose themselves or someone they love to such physical suffering? There *are* natural and healthy ways of avoiding pregnancy. The natural methods involve both the man and woman in the learning process, unlike contraception, where the burden usually falls solely on the woman.

3. Beside the physical and emotional effects, particularly on the woman, the contraceptive sexual act is, knowingly or unknowingly, dishonest. It doesn't speak the truth of the act. With contraceptive sex, our bodies say, "I'm totally yours." But in reality this is not true because, in this case, we are holding back our fertility. "The physical union is meant to express a personal union. Sexual intimacy is an expression of total love, total trust, total commitment. In giving their bodies to each other, couples are giving their very selves to each other."[21] The contraceptive act does not express this totality.

---

[20] Ann Pietrangelo, "The Effects of Hormonal Birth Control on Your Body," updated September 9, 2020, https://www.healthline.com/health/birth-control-effects-on-body. One last important fact to remember is that contraception is not 100% effective, even with the best that the market has. See https://www.cdc.gov/reproductivehealth/UnintendedPregnancy/PDF/Contraceptive_methods_508.pdf.

[21] Edward Sri, *Love Unveiled* (San Francisco: Ignatius Press, 2015), 251.

CHAPTER 4

Twelve Common Fears About Relationships

FEAR IS A COMMON EMOTION felt in dating due to natural expectations we might have toward the other. Fears can paralyze, confuse, and stifle confidence in dating relationships. Hence, it is good to assess such fears in your life and in your relationships. Below are some typical fears that one might experience.

1. **Fear of losing ultimate happiness.** Will this person be able to make me happy for the rest of my life? This is a fundamentally incorrect view of any relationship, even marriage. It is based on the erroneous idea of loving as "taking" versus "giving." How can this person *make me* happy? Love is a two-way street. It is also erroneous to think another imperfect human being will make me happy. **Yes, another person can add to your happiness,**

for sure, but we need to be very realistic about the limitations of another person to fulfill all our needs. They can't. We must also remember that perfect happiness is not something promised us in this life. We will have to wait for it to be attained in heaven.

2. **Fear of not being enough.** The more one learns about me, the less he or she will like me. Everyone battles with personal insecurities. This one tops the list for most people. Am I good enough and do I deserve their love? Perceived self-worth today is often based on the material and social. For a woman, it is often her circle of friends, what kind of body she has, or questioning her own desirability. For a man, it is often what job he holds, how much money he makes, what he owns, or his trophy girlfriend or wife. We have to be very careful of measuring ourselves according to these materialistic standards. Our ultimate value comes from our dignity in being made in the image of an all-loving Creator.

3. **Fear of settling for someone.** As one learns more about the other person, the less one is actually convinced they should be together. When you begin spending time with one person, everything is exposed: the good, the bad, and the ugly. Make a non-negotiable list of what you desire in a relationship. If some of those more critical points are not lining up, then it's time to talk and maybe even say goodbye. This is why they are called non-negotiables. You cannot move forward unless both parties are clear regarding the non-negotiables.

4. **Fear of being too subjective in the relationship.** There is a danger in not seeing the relationship clearly and not being able to evaluate if it is good. The lack of objectivity or being blinded by one's own subjective viewpoint will not help you discern important choices in dating. This is where good friends and close family members come into the picture. We need people around us who care about us and who, for our own good, are capable of telling us things that we either cannot see or do not want to hear.

5. **Fear of the other using me.** Will the other person take advantage of me after I give them "everything"? This is a very common concern in our narcissistic culture. Sexual promiscuity, for example, nurtures a *using mentality* toward the other. On the other hand, this *using mentality* has other expressions. While one party is doing all the giving, the other is doing all the receiving. The party who is giving tries to see past the selfish behavior, excusing the other, and trying to focus on the good. Yet, the moment comes when serious doubt sets in because such "goodwill giving" can be abused by the other party and is rarely reciprocated.

6. **Fear of hurting the other.** Will my bad habits, selfish tendencies, or lack of self-giving push him/her away? The reality of our own inadequacies can often overwhelm us. Women in particular can fall into a constant questioning of themselves, their gifts, qualities, lack of qualities, and the list goes on. These tendencies can come from

an unhealthy perfectionism[22] and can lead to more angst in the relationship and an unhealthy cycle of self-questioning. Men, on the other hand, desire physical intimacy *in the moment*, and hurting the other is not their objective. Nevertheless, it often *does* hurt. The truth is that men, in their mental wiring, do not feel the emotional impact of sexual intimacy as women do. In fact, they can be very callous. One area of hurt that often goes unaddressed is an unplanned pregnancy that results from sexual intercourse. In this case, the brunt of the hurt falls upon the woman who bears the child.

7. **Fear of being rejected.** What will they say when I open up about my past? This is a concern based on vulnerability. How will the other see and judge our fears and insecurities? This is a very real concern because everybody has a personal history. Bad choices from the past can bring emotional and psychological wounds that can have serious personal consequences. There is also the question of how much we tell them. Do they need to know everything? These are important questions that merit reflection, but also confidence in the other. If this person is really the one for you, then moments of shared vulnerability usually bring a deeper level of trust. Finally, it's important to mention the value of *patience*. A lot of patience is key because both parties will need time to grow to a level of trust to be able to open up about such personal issues.

---

[22] Such perfectionism can come from one's own temperament or from the negative influence of social media.

8. **Fear of a lifestyle change.** Will this relationship force a change to my lifestyle? "I like my life right now." There is often a tendency of avoiding being in a relationship when you are accustomed to, and identify comfortably with, being single. Will you lose your care-free lifestyle? Accountability to another person, in its different forms, can cause fear and may paralyze you into not committing.

9. **Fear of having to change oneself for the other.** Going from "me" to "us." Will this person try to change me? Any healthy relationship is about changing yourself for the better. However, when you change yourself to make the other happy, and yet know deep down "this is not really me," then there can be negative consequences. For example, trying to change the other's values on important principles they live by, like whether one practices a faith or not or drinks too much or too little or even practices proper self-care or not. The way to overcome the fear of change is to *begin with the end in mind*. Ask yourself: "What steps do I need to take in order to arrive at where I ultimately want to be in my life? What kind of person will help me get there?" Overcoming and letting go of fears related to changes in yourself will be necessary in order to take a step forward toward long-term fulfillment and happiness.

10. **Fear of being controlling with the other.** "What if I come on too strong?" This fear is common for people who struggle with patience in the relationship. Things

need to progress naturally. If you think you are moving too fast in the relationship, it is probably because you are. However, if you find yourself getting anxious, then you either need to share that with the one you are dating or get objective advice from a trusted friend. "What is causing me to be so restless?" Both parties should know when the relationship is moving into "deeper waters" and be willing to talk about it.

11. **Fear of doing the right thing.** "Will I be strong enough to break up the relationship if it needs to happen?" Dating is for assessing and then, at times, "dumping." Every dating relationship will end in either getting married or breaking up. Needless to say, if you end up dating several different people before getting married, then you will go through several breakups before marriage. Most of the suffering comes when we do not want to hurt the other and delay too long before finally ending it. Problems with pulling away from a relationship may also be due to the fact you are having sex. Keep this in mind as you date: the less physical you get with someone, the easier it will be to break up if/when you need to. The more physically intimate you get, the more painful it will be to break up. If you want to gain clarity of mind in order to see the relationship *as it really is* and take action, then the first thing to do is to pull back on the physical intimacy. Sexual intercourse releases oxytocin which creates a bond between two people. One of the reasons that sexual intimacy is for marriage is precisely this: our very biology is wired to keep

a couple together (primarily for the sake of children). The effect of the oxytocin hormone proves it.

12. **Fear of not being able to be alone.** Being single again after dating is not simply "getting over someone." It is also learning how to adapt to a new lifestyle. It is also often necessary to avoid communication with that person you once dated. It is not easy to be alone after a relationship, but it shows how prepared we are for love. If being alone is hard, it is best for us not to date right now. Sometimes the fear of being alone is a consequence of us avoiding the need for more personal growth. Post-relationship "crisis" can afford a unique moment to pause and do some much-needed introspection on goals and purpose instead of diving immediately into yet another relationship.

In the end, if you begin dating with a mutual understanding about openness and honesty, then such fears will never grow enough to consume you. We insist on the need for quiet time for personal reflection because only then can one identify from where such fears come. There is a popular passage in the Bible: "There is no fear in love, but perfect love casts out fear." (1 John 4:18 *NRSV*) When thoughts about the future scare us, we are usually not including God. He wants to hear about our fears, and we do not often include Him. The same God that allows us to overcome present uncertainties sometimes strangely does not factor into our future. "Peace I leave with you, my peace I give to you." (John 14:27 *NRSV*) It is true peace He desires for us. So, seek out more prayerful silence and solitude in your life to find that peace that only God can bring.

THE PROBLEM OF COMMITMENT

1. In modern relationships, there exists a practice of new couples deleting their dating apps together. It appears to be a *rite of passage* in modern relationships. Alternately, keeping the dating apps active while still in a relationship implies that one or both parties seem to prefer "not being tied down" by commitment. There is, in this case, a reluctance to commit.[23] They want to keep their options open. When every feature of your life is customizable with simply a swipe or a click, why would you tie yourself down, right? Freedom is an absolute value today. Leaving your options *open* is an imperative. This concept of freedom is so unqualified, and personal independence so absolute, that any guidelines which are in the least bit normative are perceived as negative and obstructing our freedom to choose. The *perceived* loss of freedom, nonetheless, seems to be the only point of reference nowadays when it comes to committing to marriage.[24] It is even worse when it comes to openness to having children!

---

[23] Bobbie Franklin, *The Problem with Millennials: Commitment*, January 29, 2018, https://lovebobbielynn.wordpress.com/2018/01/28/the-problem-with-millenials-commitment.

[24] Professor's House, *Single Versus Married Life - Pro's and Con's*, December, 2017, https://www.professorshouse.com/single-versus-married-life.

2. The "absolutizing" of freedom seems to play out in a new "model" of marriage. This model assumes that a long-term commitment, like marriage, should last only as long as it remains happy, fulfilling, and life-giving to the self. Marriage is *only* for so long as "our love shall last" — where "love" is understood as feeling fulfilled, happy, or self-actualized. This does not include raising children, running a household, establishing a measure of financial security, or giving support to one's spouse and kin (as well as possibly receiving it). Yet, according to research, going into marriage endorsing this attitude only increases the chance of divorce as compared to husbands and wives who take the view that "divorce is not an option."[25]

> **Why does our society seem to demoralize marriage and family life by focusing solely on the sacrifices and struggles? There is much joy to be had, yet many miss out because they fall for this prejudice. We need to be reminded of the positives.**

3. Commitment *is* a good thing. Every choice brings with it some type of sacrifice—something you *did not* choose and have to give up. Choices commit you especially in a relationship. You cannot get around it. Hence, this

---

[25] Institute for Family Studies, *State of Contradiction*, 2020, https://if-studies.org/ifs-admin/resources/ifs-stateofcontradiction-final-1.pdf. It is inherently selfish to say, "I'll only stay with you as long as you make me happy."

current spirit of absolute freedom is based on a lie. It does not really exist. Serious dating is a commitment to a beneficial personal end for *both* parties. You are called to give the best of yourself to another and *both* will benefit. As one dating blogger expressed it well: "Commitment [in dating] carries risk. You could get hurt or rejected or lose out on meeting someone just a little better-looking or with a higher salary. Your friend might not be there for you when you've been there for them. However, when you commit, you have a lot to gain. Because when you commit, your passion and love show. I think that's beauty."[26]

4. Marriage is the fullest expression of the beauty of committed love. When one commits to another person in marriage, certain freedoms are sacrificed yet other goods are acquired. We *do* win in marriage. It *does* bring important benefits to each party. Marriage simply makes the other a better person. It is the perfecting of one's love for the other, from selfish to more selfless. On average, married people have greater overall happiness and actually have more sex (and better-quality sex) than people who do not marry.[27] Does this sound like something you might want?

---

[26] Ibid.

[27] Hilary White, "*Marriage More Mutually Beneficial than Living Together, British Study Determines,*" https://www.lifesitenews.com/news/marriage-more-mutually-beneficial-than-living-together-british-study-determ; Nathan Yau, "*Married People Have More Sex,*" https://flowingdata.com/2017/07/03/married-people-sex.

CHAPTER

Healthy Boundaries in Dating[28]

1. All relationships, including friendships, siblings, lovers, and business relations, need boundaries. In dating, it is the responsibility of *both parties* to consider this important point. On some level, all "boundary-setting" means is saying "no" to some things and also saying "yes" to some things. Boundaries promote our sense of "self" and help us preserve personal integrity while also creating a framework for our relationships. How can we avoid the pitfalls of disrespect and manipulation while choosing mutual respect for each other? Boundaries. We should aspire to the values that protect and develop the relationship. Couples need to prioritize boundary setting

---

28 Connor LC, *Reclaiming Love*, 44.

to protect the integrity of the relationship. However, many couples ignore the need for boundaries. If you have chronic feelings of resentment, anger, manipulation, or being treated as unimportant, you definitely need to set some boundaries in your relationship.

2. Any couple who is willing to set boundaries is saying something very important to the other. They are creating a need to communicate about something that defines their values, and they should do so early on in their relationship. The famous series on boundaries by Drs. Cloud and Townsend sums up well what defines a boundary:

> *"Simply put, a boundary is a **property line**. Just as a physical fence marks out where your yard ends and your neighbors begin, a personal boundary distinguishes what is your emotional world or personal property, and what belongs to someone else. You can't see your own boundary. However, you can tell it is there when someone crosses it. When another person tries to control you, tries to get close to you, or asks you to do something you don't think is right, you should feel some sense of protest. Your boundary has been crossed."*[29]

3. Boundaries define us by showing what we are and what we are not. When we are clear about our values

---

[29] Henry Cloud and John Townsend, *Boundaries in Dating* (Grand Rapids MI: Zondervan, 2000), 28.

and motivations, we can avoid many problems before they even start. Another definition of a boundary is a "qualified no" that says what, where, when, and under what circumstances you will engage or not engage with the other person. Boundaries also *protect* us by letting others know what we will and will not tolerate. One party says "no" because they care about the other. By doing so, you are forcing the other person to intentionally state the purpose of their actions and detach themselves from any unhealthy behavior because you love them.

IMPORTANT PREREQUISITES FOR EFFECTIVE BOUNDARIES

1. We have a mutual **good** or goal in this relationship, and we need to cooperate with each other to protect it.

2. Violations of this good, or any acts that go against it, are harmful to both of us. Infractions should be seen as doing harm to oneself *and* to the other since the mutual agreement was to strive to help lift each other up.

FIVE STEPS TO SETTING BOUNDARIES IN YOUR RELATIONSHIP[30]

1. **Choose to set boundaries.** One only tolerates a difficult relationship situation as long as they choose to tolerate it. You get what you tolerate. Be confident and choose to set

---

[30] Jacqueline, "*Boundaries in Romantic Relationships*," November 8, 2016, https://cyberparent.com/relationships/boundaries-in-romantic-relationships.

boundaries. The sooner the better. It does not matter what has happened in the past. It is never too late. Today is a new day.

2. **Identify the source of conflict and hurt.** It often takes some real soul-searching to figure out the source of anger or resentment. "We *can* do something about this awkward tension between us." Identifying *what* exactly causes the tension will help identify the boundary needed.

3. **Decide where to set the boundaries.** Think about the entire situation. Consider your time, emotions, and means. Then, consider whether you are helping the other person or merely allowing them to avoid or postpone his/her own problem-solving. Try to help the other person without taking on the whole problem.

4. **Express the boundaries clearly.** Boundaries come in all kinds of forms (see below). An example would be when one party says to the other, "I prefer to not be pushed further sexually because it is against my beliefs."

5. **Stick to *your* boundaries.** You are not responsible for making the other person obey the boundaries. You are only responsible for following the boundaries yourself and for reinforcing them. There can be a lot of emotion tied up in sticking to your boundaries. However, both parties need to strive to enforce the agreed upon boundaries and remind the other of their importance. The consequences

of broken boundaries must be laid out clearly as an indication of their importance.

UNDERSTANDING BOUNDARIES

1. Boundaries can touch on many aspects of the relationships. Physical boundaries, for example, are of consequence due to the negative repercussions of physical intimacy when introduced too soon.[31] If your head is clouded by passion or other non-essential influences, then the "essentials" will be lost. The premium put on physical attraction today dominates the dating landscape to the demise of other essentials such as a happy, fulfilling relationships. Rather than looking at boundaries as something negative or a deficiency, boundaries highlight our unique gift as human beings to be able to consciously identify a personal need and then safeguard it. We can be thoughtful and introspective and not just react to impulses.

2. What is important to know is that *there is freedom to choose* at this stage of love. Therefore, we are free to choose to respond or to not respond. If boundaries in a romantic relationship are respected, other areas of your relationship will be respected. There is a direct correlation here because respectful behavior communicates, "I am listening to you, I acknowledge you, and I want what's best for

---

[31] Chris Iliades, "*Is There a Price to Pay for Promiscuity?*", July 15, 2010, https://www.everydayhealth.com/longevity/can-promiscuity-threaten-longevity.aspx.

you." Nonetheless, the culture has determined that our emotional world is just something that spontaneously moves us, like being bumped around on a subway without choosing it. This translates very quickly into "it's outside of our responsibility, even our conscience, to say no to following this intense emotion."

EMOTIONAL BOUNDARIES

1. The early stages of dating demand more emotional boundaries. Remember that at early stages of dating, you are only learning about this person and the possibility of mutual compatibility. Control the tendency to "tell all" and do not run too quickly to the other with problems about friends or family.[32]

2. Spending too much time with each other is unrealistic and excessive. Such behavior expresses too much emotional investment than is necessary (or healthy) in the early stages of dating. Many times, married life is not even like this. For example, non-stop texting is waste of time and

---

[32] *Throwing* yourself into a new relationship may reflect emotional immaturity: "I am really lonely" or "I need his/her affection to feel good about myself." Obsessiveness reflects someone out of balance usually caused by some deeper insecurity or negative experience.

harmful to a relationship. It is empty and just distracts you from the present moment.

Josie, 25, dating, Occupational Therapist

"Emotional boundaries are valuable in a relationship. It is important for young adults to solve their problems on their own as much as possible before dumping them on their significant other. Being overly vulnerable shows immaturity when it takes place in a dating-stage in which it is more appropriate for the individual to be taking care of him or herself."

VERBAL BOUNDARIES

1. Words have meaning. Words have power. Love is a very strong word and is too easily thrown around. It should be protected. Be careful not to introduce pet names or strong words too quickly like "love of my life" or "babe" or "honey" until a more advanced stage of commitment is ***imminent***. Such language "plays up" the sense of a more permanent relationship of which dating is ***not.***

2. Talking about sexual things (jokes, innuendos, hypothetical situations). Sexual intimacy is life-giving and sacred. It is not merely *recreational*. Once you go there, it opens up the facility of belittling what should be honored. Did you know that marriage vows are renewed with each act of sexual intimacy? Yet, if you are not married, what are you renewing?

Marie, 27, single, Advertising

"Wow I have so many comments about this. A guy I was in love with when in college said through the grapevine that "Marie is the love of his life and I'd love to marry her someday, but she's way too good for me." I confronted him about it, so I know it was true. I still remember every detail about where I was standing, who said it, every word verbatim, and how I felt. I don't think guys truly realize that they must be very prudent in words with their significant other. It's super harmful for women."

PHYSICAL BOUNDARIES

1. People are all different and can be aroused in different ways. Know each other's personal triggers, not to exploit them but to protect them. Is "anything but sex" the right attitude?

2. The case of kissing is one that fits here. Passionate kissing can be a trigger for erotic desire. The proper place for such desires to play out is within the commitment of marriage, not dating. Both self-restraint and caution need to be exercised when it comes to kissing because it so quickly leads to more physical displays of affection.

3. Examples of physical boundaries include putting limits on drinking together, a curfew for hanging out at night, healthy choices of movies/entertainment, limits on spending too much time together, and cuddling for extended time (side-lying).

4. If this person is not your future spouse, would you feel comfortable sharing what you have done with this person with your future spouse? (or any person you have dated for that matter?)[33]

5. Wearing revealing clothing while around the person who desires to know you more deeply can often hinder them from focusing on you as a person.

Colton Underwood, newest star of "The Bachelor," former linebacker for the San Diego Chargers, on waiting for marriage:

"Let's hope that there's more to it than just the virginity thing." "But it's not up for me to prove anything or have to defend it, but I think if people are looking for more clarity on it, or more background on it, they're definitely going to get that."… "It's just a lot of things that go into it. It's not a simple answer."

DIGITAL BOUNDARIES

1. All relationships today will need *digital detoxing*. Beware of thinking that digital connection is real human communication. It is and it is not. In a committed relationship where true intimacy is forged, the less artificial it is, the better and the digital world can be so artificial. Couples instinctively know this but are often numbed by habit. The digital world is so mentally intrusive that it brings about a real resistance to thinking and

---

[33] Consider the opposite: If this person *does* become your spouse, then what story do you want to be able to tell your children? "Your mom and dad waited until marriage and it's been beautiful, so you should do this, too."

communicating, and therefore connecting deeply with the other. Set personal and couple boundaries on your use of social media. This might be the #1 obstacle for any couple really wanting to grow together.

2. **Suggestions:** Pick moments during the week/month where you do a "digital-fast."[34] Be accountable to one another in your commitment. Commit to activities that intentionally avoid forms of digital distraction: go for a walk with no phones, indulge in an even longer trek during the weekend, go to Church together with no phones, or drive with no music in the car (at least part of the time).

CROSSING BOUNDARIES

1. **Once boundaries are established; they will need *revisiting* when they are crossed.** Love is based on the good of the other. Clear and honest recognition is needed to identify both *when* the boundary is crossed and *how* this action taints the "mutual good" of the couple through the misdeed of self-interest. It is important that these infractions are not glossed over, but clearly recognized as selfish and not seeking the good of the other. Given how our culture exploits the human body, especially that of women, men will need to say the words "I respect you" often. Doing so helps counter the selfish response of a broken boundary, "I am just expressing love and

---

[34] Exodus 90 or Fiat 90 ascesis programs can help bring more balance into your digital world.

affection." Simply be candid and matter of fact. Accept failure, ask for forgiveness, and move on. If you say you respect me, what are you actually doing about it? **Words and actions need to be one and the same thing.**

2. Because attraction arouses sensual desire, it can impel people very powerfully towards forms of intimacy. Some may say, "What's wrong with that? It's natural." The answer is: Human beings are more than instinctual animals; We have the capacity to reason. We know intuitively that if fleeting instinctual pleasure brought happiness, the world would sparkle like the sun at least half the time. Yet, rather than creating more fulfilling relationships, we see how pain and brokenness abound when the gratification of our selfish wants rules. The "evil" of lust is just that, evil. It is contrary to the truth and goodness of the other person. As St. Francis de Sales once said, "Take care to admit no evil love because you will soon become evil yourself." Love demands investment *in the person*, and therefore is never merely an erotic desire. It doesn't matter whether the relationship is romantic or not. *Boundaries,* by Drs. Cloud and Townsend, states the clear dangers of lust: "Just like a drug addict is not growing when he or she is using drugs, your soul is not growing if you are acting out of lust… Passionate lust splits your real heart, your mind, your values, and the life that you truly desire."[35]

---

[35] Cloud and Townsend, *Boundaries in Dating*, 249.

QUESTIONS TO ASK IN THE EARLY STAGES OF DATING

Women:

- Do you feel safe with him physically?
- Is he protecting you in his actions?
- At the very least, if/when you present certain boundaries for your relationship, does he respond by respecting them?
- Do you think he is too aggressive? Has he said he struggles with lust or has alluded to it (i.e., commenting "out loud" on other attractive women)?
- Does he stop a situation from getting too physical as often as you do?
- Does he set boundaries too? Does he take initiative? (A girl should be looking for a guy who will sacrifice his desires *for her protection.)*
- How are you helping or not helping him protect you from being objectified?

Men:

- Does she make you better? Does she set boundaries with you? Do you see this as an equal responsibility?
- Is this person bringing you closer to or farther away from being who God wants you to be?
- Do you feel uncomfortable with her physically?
- Do you think she is too aggressive? Has she said she struggles with lust or has alluded to it?
- Does she encourage you to fall into lust with the way that she dresses or the situations she leads you into?

- How are you helping to stop these situations from coming about in the first place? Do you understand your role as protector?

3. Setting boundaries is very challenging. It often seems an insurmountable task when love is involved. However, like all "people skills," setting boundaries is a process that gets easier with practice. Like the faded lines on a baseball field, we need to frequently *redefine the lines* so that we know where and when we are out of bounds and so the players in the game know where to run. It's often the case with boundaries that people do not reap the benefits in the short term, but only when time passes. They are always grateful for such honest conversations.

CHAPTER 6

Pornography: Why is This Subject Here?

1. If you have not encountered this issue in your personal or dating life, consider yourself extremely fortunate. One study recommends wisely, "When couples decide to work on their relationship issues, pornography needs to be approached thoughtfully. Couples need to understand each other's beliefs and attitudes. If there are major gaps in how they view pornography, it is going to be difficult to discuss sexuality and the relationship in general without coming to some consensus about those conflicts… couples may also differ in whether they see porn use as infidelity. One person may see themselves as being innocent of any transgression, while the other feels betrayed."[36] In general,

---

[36] Grant Hillary Brenner, *"When is Porn Use a Problem?"*, February 19, 2018, https://www.psychologytoday.com/us/blog/experimentations/201802/when-is-porn-use-problem.

people can get very defensive, even combative, about this issue. It's particularly so with men. Understanding and mastering this issue before initiating any relationship is an intelligent thing to do.

2. The effects of this serious, social issue are profoundly evident in the behavior of men and women alike. One SA director (Sexaholics Anonymous) describes the common effects in men as sounding like, "I no longer feel an emotional response to anything," "There is nothing in my life I enjoy doing," "I feel totally isolated from the world," "My anxiety and stress levels are at an all-time high."[37] After a 10-year battle herself, one girl relates that "pornography is our mind-warping way to find emotional and physical fulfillment in a past incident between strangers we see on a screen. People become like objects. Relationships become a cesspit of using, abuse, self-gratification, temporariness, and substitutions. Monogamy seems less than fulfilling."[38]

3. The latest evidence of the toxic effects of pornography is astounding.[39] This is exactly why this subject was suddenly inserted, particularly in the early stages of dating. It is not

---

[37] Ann Tolley, *10 Toxic Side Effects from Pornography Use*, https://www.familytoday.com/relationships/10-toxic-side-effects-of-pornography-use.

[38] Sheila Wray Gregoire, "*Top 10 Things to Know About Women and Porn Addiction*," May 24, 2016, https://tolovehonorandvacuum.com/2016/05/women-porn-addiction.

[39] See https://www.covenanteyes.com for all the latest statistics on pornography.

something that can be overlooked, especially as the negative consequences grow in long-term relationships. How does it affect people exactly?[40] Let's list out a few examples:

- Pornography conditions the viewer to expect constant sexual novelty, so arousal generally declines with the same mate. Only those who regularly found different mates were able to continue their arousal.
- Those who watch pornography regularly admit to feeling dominated by their own sexual desires.
- Studies show that the brains of pornography addicts look exactly like those of drug addicts. This is now common knowledge.
- Other typical negative effects: premature ejaculation, disinterest in sex with their partner, difficulty reaching orgasm, and erectile dysfunction.

4. The objectification of another person for one's personal gratification is the direct opposite of love. Love is the heart of any healthy relationship. Do not underestimate the *pornification* of the culture and its effects, directly or indirectly, in your life.

5. If one is currently struggling with pornography, it is very likely that he/she will fall into one of two categories. The first category is that one believes that he/she will be able to

---

[40] Scott Christian, *"10 Reasons Why You Should Quit Watching Porn,"* November 20, 2013, https://www.gq.com/story/10-reasons-why-you-should-quit-watching-porn.

quit whenever they please or that if not now, at some point in the future, maybe once you are in a relationship or married. The second category is one who already believes that he/she must quit and have tried and failed to stop many times. They are now dealing with all the shame and guilt that comes along with it. If you belong to the first group and believe that there is no problem or that you will stop later, then ***do it***! Go six months without using. Most will probably not last a week. If one can, great! Count yourself fortunate and take stock. Is your life better, has your emotional state improved or confidence increased? If one cannot stop, then he/she will soon find themselves a member of the second group.

6. Belonging to the second category means one honestly wants to be free. Please be kind to yourself. It is truly one of the great tragedies of our time that so many must suffer from this addiction. Please take hope in these words of former addict Matt Talbot: "Never be too hard on the man who can't give up, it's as hard to give up drink as it is to raise the dead to life again. But both are possible and even easy for our Lord. We have only to depend on him."

THE FACTS

1. There is a great deal of controversy from medical professionals on where compulsion ends and addiction begins. Regardless, people can suffer with any form of exposure to pornography and, whether addiction or compulsion, people still need help. Pornography is also not just a "guy thing"; more women than ever are viewing it. One of the world's most popular free sites, Pornhub, which is visited by 115 million people per day, recently revealed that women make up *a quarter* of its global audience. The data shows that, for women, watching pornography is mostly a solo adventure and that it goes down considerably once in a long-term relationship.[41] Whether you stay with this person or not, you will be helping them, and, in most cases, you are helping one another just by talking about it.

2. Here are a few facts from 2018[42] about pornography that undermine the development of love in dating (or really any relationship):

- 90% of teens and 96% of young adults are either encouraging, accepting, or neutral when they talk about pornography with their friends.
- 51% of male students and 32% of female students first viewed pornography before their teenage years.
- The first age of exposure to pornography on average for both boys and girls is around 13 years old.
- 56% of divorces involved one party having an obsessive interest in pornography.

---

[41] Dawn Michael, *"Why Women are Watching More Porn Than Ever Before,"* January 31, 2018, https://www.yourtango.com/experts/dawn-michael/women-watch-porn-fantasies.

[42] Covenant Eyes, https://www.covenanteyes.com.

Striking words from celebrated Author and Feminist, Naomi Wolf:

"The young women who talk to me on campuses about the effect of pornography on their intimate lives speak of feeling that they can never measure up, that they can never ask for what they want; and that if they do not offer what porn offers, they cannot expect to hold a guy. The young men talk about what it is like to grow up learning about sex from porn, and how it is not helpful to them in trying to figure out how to be with a real woman... For the first time in human history, the images' power and allure have supplanted that of real naked women. Today, real naked women are just bad porn."

3. Pornography use is difficult to hide. Here are some signs that might indicate a possible struggle:[43]

- Defensiveness or anger when asked about the subject.
- Becoming physically aggressive and pushing physical boundaries.
- Not letting you see their phone when asked; the search engine is frequently clean.
- Nervous reactions when you surprise them and they are on their phone.
- Strongly reacting to roommates that open the bedroom door unexpectedly.
- Noticeably distracted; often irritable or moody.
- The completion of other vital life tasks is not happening. It appears that something is interfering with normal daily activity.

---

[43] Northpoint Washington, "*11 Signs You May Be Addicted to Pornography*," May 27, 2019, https://www.northpointwashington.com/blog/11-signs-may-addicted-porn.

WHEN DO WE HAVE THIS CONVERSATION?

1. Some say right away, others say give it some time. One way to gauge that moment is when *consistent* behavior on both sides indicates: "I am *very* interested in you and I want you to know me." **Trust** is the bedrock of a good relationship. With porn use, like any substance abuse disorder, minimizing the issue and dishonesty are often the norm and quite often include duplicitous behavior (a double life) which kills trust.

2. Each person needs to determine the timeline of this conversation depending on how strongly you feel about the issue. This book advocates that the conversation should happen *earlier* rather than later. Nonetheless, let's be crystal clear: **this subject MUST be addressed at some point in a dating relationship**.

3. Due to the shame that comes with this behavior, it is not going to be on the "Top 10" list of desired conversations. However, it is crucial that it comes up. Most men, for example, will be reluctant to bring this subject up unless forced to.[44] Besides this, if they are asked to give specifics, they *might avoid details or minimize the issue altogether.* Most people minimize the issue in their life and are not completely open.

---

[44] Men, in particular, can't fathom how talking about it will help. They think that any mention of it as a problem will end the relationship; that they will not be accepted but rejected.

4. Given the sensitive nature of the theme, and to avoid putting the other in a situation of possible dishonesty, here are some ideas to help broach the subject:

- Possible opening line: *"Hey, I need to know where you are on the topic of pornography. I want to make sure we are helping one another."*
- This manner of initiating the theme assumes that it *is* an issue. Right now, the statistics are in favor of this assumption so why not just "put it out there?" You are making a judgment on what healthy human behavior is and *not* necessarily judging the other person. Avoiding a judgmental spirit cannot be stressed enough because of the hypersensitivity of shame around this struggle.
- If either party (or both) admits *"Yes, I have had issues,"* then how can one "interpret" such a yes without more invasive questioning? Questions like, "" "*how long have you struggled with it,*" "*how frequently does it happen*," and "*what is the current status*" are all very valid questions but can become too accusatory in tone and shut down openness.
- *"Yes, I have issues,"* as in, "*right now I am battling with it."* could mean one of two things: a) "*yes I am addicted*" or b) "*yes I have a compulsion to use it.*"
- *"Yes, I had issues, but not so much now".* This also can mean many things but usually either: a) *"I fell often in the past but now less frequently, maybe every month or so"* or b) "*I looked at pornography in the past, but now I haven't fallen in a long time (like months)."*

- Either response above merits two very important follow-up questions: *"What are you (or we) doing right now to overcome it?"* and *"How can I help you?"*

KEY SIGNS OF TRUE SINCERITY IN OVERCOMING THE ISSUE

1. To the possible responses given above, it is vital to be able to recognize whether there is a sincere intention to overcome this issue. Bottom line: **Sincerity** must translate into "action" not empty promises or even good intentions. The person or couple needs to show the other that they are taking steps to overcome the struggle. If one cannot point to concrete things that he or she has done to address this issue, then they are deceiving themselves. The person in question needs to be accountable *to someone.*[45]

   All too often a person battling with such issues has made "solemn" promises that "today will be the last day," that they "will never go back" only to fall again. If their method is not getting them the desired results, it means that they need to try something new. One will be able to tell if their solution is working or not within a short period of time.

2. That someone is preferably not the questioning party (as if they are some sort of therapist or counselor) because this

---

[45] It is recommended that, if you are dating or married to someone who struggles with this issue, it is best that your significant other is not the accountability partner. They should know about the issue and when you fall. However, it is suggested that the person in question have a friend who is of the same sex to hold them accountable.

can cause more harm than good. Repeatedly listening to your significant other about this issue (essentially that they were desiring someone else) will literally tear the other apart. It will be important that they do speak to someone, but, if the revelations cause pain, it will be more difficult for them to be honest. Remember, we are in a dating relationship. This is not marriage. You have no obligation to remain dating the person. Does one completely abandon the other? Of course not. The conversation and efforts made up to this point are meant to encourage honesty in a true spirit of kindness and compassion.

3. Forms of accountability are common practice for all recovery treatments. Here are some questions illustrating some forms of accountability:

- Do they have some protection on their phone/tablet/ computer that blocks such undesirable exposure? What needs to take place to make this happen?
- Is there anyone in their life (besides you) that knows they struggle with this and wants to help them? (This is based on the wise principle that an honest open confession with others brings peace and the confidence to seek help).
- Are they part of any small group with others to help them stay honest with themselves? (This can take the form of an Sexaholics Anonymous group, book study, bible study, prayer group, sports team, etc.)

- If this has been going on for a while, have they sought out professional help?[46]
- What kind of spiritual support have they received? (For Catholics: prayer, confession, spiritual direction).

If you have discussed this theme openly, then a period of time should be allowed for one to prove their sincerity in overcoming the issue. A concrete plan is important.

WHEN IS ENOUGH ENOUGH? WHEN THIS ISSUE ENDS THE RELATIONSHIP

1. One important fact to remember is that healing this addiction takes time and a lot of hard work. Very rarely does the change come from just saying, *"I will stop."* Besides this, the response, *"I used to have a problem"* (but not anymore), comes with the clear caveat that it is quite likely that they will fall again. This is the *nature of the beast.* Human nature often brings us back to our "puddle" of misery. Hence, this is why it is so important to see concrete

---

[46] See Chapter Eleven for resources on this issue and others.

steps being taken to overcome the issue. Otherwise, it is truly just wishful thinking. One should withdraw from further physical and emotional advancement if the other is not making progress.

2. Should you consider marrying someone who has a pornography issue?[47]

Trust is the hallmark of any good relationship, particularly one such as marriage. This type of commitment is too important and exclusive to accept anything less. To enter into a marriage with a man or woman who's cultivating desires for someone beyond the one who they are with or married to is simply too dangerous. The need to be in a relationship with a man or woman who is cultivating exclusive desires for you is key to renewing trust. The following signs are a clear indication that there is a real insincerity in overcoming the problem:

- If the conversation on this issue seems to get frequently deflected or downplayed.
- If you are catching them in repeated lies.[48]
- If the troubling signs mentioned above continue to appear in their behavior.

---

[47] Would you marry someone who has an alcohol issue? A drug issue? If you're a slave to anything, then you are not free enough to give the best of yourself to your spouse. You need to break free first before you can consider taking on deeper commitments like marriage.

[48] If you choose to stay in the relationship, the only response to chronic lying is to demand that they see a therapist or give some real proof that they are seeing one.

- If none of the forms of accountability mentioned are in place in the person's life after a reasonable period of time has passed.

3. After an agreed amount of time has passed, if any of these signs above are present, in most cases it will spell insincerity. Studies show that if such insincerity goes unchecked, the problem will only get worse. If they cannot own this issue with honesty and openness toward you **now** while you are dating, it is quite likely this pattern of behavior will continue even into marriage. It will, perhaps, show up in other important issues as well. This will only sow distrust which is devastating to any relationship.

4. Given the current crisis of love, it is also important to name the extreme opposite to life-giving love: self-eroticism. Masturbation is the attempt to find pleasure and happiness in oneself alone rather than with others. While it seems to be "natural," studies show that masturbation can become highly addictive and create personal alienation, self-loathing, a depletion of one's interpersonal skills, and is dangerous to one's overall health.[49] Along with a cultural epidemic, such as pornography, comes the mentality that somehow this isolated act doesn't hurt anyone. This

---

[49] Jason Vredenburg, Performance Insiders, "What are the Side Effects of Excessive Masturbation?", February 20, 2019, https://www. performanceinsiders.com/excessive-masturbation-side-effects.html. One example is erectile dysfunction. Thirty million men suffer from it. There are many causes of erectile dysfunction and one of them is excess masturbation.

is false. Since *love is relational*, and relationships involve more than one person, one's personal choices do not affect just one individual, but the entire vista of who we are and with whom we relate (self, family, and community).[50]

5. The sexual function of the human body is meant by God to be enjoyed in "the total meaning of mutual self-giving"[51] within the marital relationship of a man and a woman. No evidence shows that masturbation prepares an adolescent or young adult for the complete gift of self in marriage or any other state in life. In fact, the self-referential, fantasy-driven nature of masturbation damages the ability to move beyond oneself and enter into mature self-giving. How can any of this be healthy for dating which should be centered on the ability to trust in healthy loving relationships?

HOW DOES PORNOGRAPHY AFFECT THE OTHER? REFLECTIONS OF A WIFE ABOUT THE ADDICTION OF HER HUSBAND[52]

1. **"It makes us feel like we are not enough."** As women, the world is constantly telling us we're not enough – not thin enough, not curvy enough, not pretty enough, not sexy enough, not sweet enough… the list goes on and on. So, when you seek out other women through pornography, you make us feel like we are not enough for you, the man

---

[50] Connor LC, *Reclaiming Love*, 85.

[51] *CCC*, 2352.

[52] The comments were offered here to help the reader see the gravity of this issue.

we chose to spend the rest of our life with. This pain is so, so deep for a woman. It's the pain of feeling totally rejected and unloved.

2. **"It makes us feel like we are an object."** If you can use women on a computer screen to pleasure yourself, then we inherently feel that's all we are to you as well – an object for your selfish desires. This robs us of our human dignity and makes marital intimacy impossible.

3. **"It hurts the whole family."** When you use pornography, it changes your personality and subconscious thoughts. I found out in my husband's disclosure that the times he was sunk deepest in pornography matched up with the times he related to me in self-centered, negative ways. In other words, you are deceiving yourself if you think you are not hurting anyone.

4. **"The deepest pain is the betrayal."** Worse than the pornography itself is the betrayal and the lies you tell us to cover it up. How can I explain this pain in a way that a man can understand? Here's an analogy: I would assume that you would never physically hit your wife, right? Well, that is the emotional equivalent of betrayal for a woman. Just because you can't see the bruises doesn't mean they aren't there. Unfortunately, in my case, my husband's betrayal is so deep that he has emotionally hit me repeatedly to the point where I have been beaten into an emotional pulp.

CHAPTER

Pursuing Life-Giving Relationships
Through the Stages of Dating

STAGE ONE: NON-EXCLUSIVE DATING – *"THINGS TO LISTEN FOR"*

1. The first dates are often filled with a lot of angst. Both parties are nervous. There is pressure to impress the other. The most important thing besides being fully present during your time together is to be a good listener. If you have not done it already, it might be good to list out the top 10 qualities that are important to you and that you seek in another person. It is important to *listen for* these qualities.

2. The following things are important to keep in mind during those first dates:

- Is there good chemistry with the other person?
- Are you attracted to them, to their "persona," not just their physical qualities or their success?
- Do you get a sense that you both have similar values regarding family, friends, faith? How do they talk about them? Positively or negatively?
- What are their motivations regarding work? Is it only about money?
- What are some things that worry you that don't jive? Are they superficial or important?

3. Find out who this person is before you invest more time and energy in the relationship. Make sure you "see" them clearly! Remember once your heart gets involved with another, then clarity of soul and mind is clouded. If you add to this romantic intensity a physical relationship, it is all the worse. The evidence proving this fact is telling[53]. When you have invested your heart in a relationship, you will not "see" and "judge" things for what they are. When the "heart-body-mind strings" are pulled, human beings often "color" the truth of reality. It is confirmation of the old saying: 'Love is blind."

---

[53] Aaron Ben Zeev, "Is Love Blind?", *Psychology Today*, March 19, 2010, https://www.psychologytoday.com/us/blog/in-the-name-love/201003/is-love-blind.

STAGE TWO: DEFINING THE RELATIONSHIP IN EXCLUSIVE DATING – *"THINGS TO LOOK FOR"*

> **Paula, 27 years old, single, medical professional**
>
> "Having the "DTR" (Defining the Relationship) conversation is important. We can't be afraid to bring up the question of where is this going? When I do so, I am caring for my own heart, mind, and emotions while being honest. So, if you're at the point of thinking "my heart is getting into this too much," be honest with yourself and with the other. In the best of cases, you'll help them segue into what their intentions are with getting to know you better, and in the worst of cases you'll be clearing the air for your relationship and protecting your heart before it gets more confusing for both of you."

1. **Some opening observations as you get to spend more time together.**

   - This may sound a bit dated, but begin by asking, "does this person exhibit *virtue*?" A virtuous person is honest and generally strives to develop good habits, such as putting others first, expressing gratitude for acts of kindness done to them, taking care of themselves, exhibiting a good work ethic and general respect for authority. These habits are not automatic and, when they appear in one's behavior, it shows a sense of good self-worth and motivation. You know what is important to someone by what they talk about and how they behave. You will see quite soon that their interactions with others express their value system. More time with that person, and especially with friends, family, and acquaintances, helps you to evaluate, as part of a continuous process of discernment, how they exhibit virtue.

Le, 31 years old, married, Federal Employee

"I have no issues with the concept of "opposites attract" but couples should have things in common too. This was precisely what attracted me to my (now) wife. We connected on so many levels."

- Another key aspect of this stage to keep in mind is that, in many cases, opposites *do* attract[54] You'll most certainly be attracted to qualities in another person that you don't have. For example, one party is disorganized, the other organized; one is friendly and outgoing, the other more reserved and quieter. How each makes decisions is also made clear: one may jump on every opportunity, the other deliberates at length over every decision. This common experience can naturally move the couple to say, "you are good for me." However, the qualities you initially *liked* in the other person can often become the ones that, in the end, really annoy you! Love is demanding. It is going to take sacrifice, accepting the other as "other." This is a huge part of marriage. Loving the other through their faults, or what you might perceive are faults, is self-giving love.

---

[54] Anastasia Tilston, "Why Do Opposites Attract? Science Finally Has the Answer," October 11, 2016, https://www.lifeadvancer.com/opposites-attract.

2. Love vs Respect: Bridging the Gender Gap[55]

- Never more than today has there been a need to foster an open and honest conversation on what gender equality means, especially in a relationship. For example, the "crisis of men" is a very real phenomenon,[56] but its solution should not come at the expense of rightful attention to women's rights and equality. We need media messages, commercials, and TV shows that portray men as responsible, competent, and caring husbands (instead of idiots and/or misogynists), just as we see an increasing number of strong, admirable women in the media. The same types of dangers exist for women. They are not being celebrated for displaying *feminine* traits (e.g., gentleness, receptivity) as consistently as for displaying more of the *masculine* traits (e.g., women superheroes being strong and fighting). These societal misconceptions contribute to the confusion. Men and women were created to both contrast and complement one another, not to clash in the center. If we fail to focus on defining men's positive roles alongside women's, we are in danger of fostering a culture of hostility.

- Today, a man's leadership in a given relationship is often considered sexist, so we'll first move to address

---

[55] Jack Myers, "The Future of Men: Masculinity in the Twenty-First Century," *Time Magazine*, May 26, 2016, https://time.com/4339209/masculinity-crisis.

[56] Ibid.

the term. A true leader is one who makes decisions, takes responsibility, and steps forward to see what needs to be done *for the good of others*. We are not talking about playing "decision maker" just for the sake of projecting leadership — a sort of "louder is better" mentality. Rather, men *should* assume some form of initiative or leadership in the relationship for the good of all parties, over and above personal self-interest! Women, in turn, need to seek this initiative from their counterpart. They want their man to be engaged, to step up and make decisions. In short, they don't want to feel like a mother to their man. Yet, few modern men actively take initiative in their relationship, and many are happy to simply be led around. In the end, mutual respect is key, but you must be wary of letting a relationship become a rudderless vessel.

- Either way, how you interact with each other becomes highly consequential later in the relationship when issues such as those concerning children, in-laws, and money come to the fore. Marriage and family life will bring real challenges and real disagreements. Does there not need to be a final decider? Beyond all this, it is important to recognize that whatever "conflict resolution" dynamic you end up using, it will spawn a thread of behavior that will continue *across your entire lifetime*. For example, if you find yourself "leading" in the relationship during this more serious dating period, then this will most likely be the consistent, long-term dynamic of your relationship. Beware of the deception that "they will change once we are married." Of course, people *can* change, but once we enter adulthood, it is generally much more difficult to change habits. Oftentimes what you see is what you get!

3. Here are some other considerations to help assess this second stage of dating:

- **Personal Interests**
  - What do they do (outside of work)? Interests and hobbies?
  - Any similar interests/hobbies?
    If the answer is very little, or they tend to be a "home-body," then it is unlikely that taking on new interests or adventures will be on their top 10 list. Do you find yourself being "you" around them? Maybe even a little silly or strange with the other and feeling at ease that you are accepted?

- **Family**
  - Closeness to family? What is their parental relationship like? Is there respect or is there a critical spirit? Is family encouraging or a source of conflict?
  - Based on the wisdom of the best psychology today, our lessons in love don't start in marriage but at home. It is good to know who was their primary caregiver: Mom or Dad? What do they like about that parent?

- *The secure bond*[57] to that primary caregiver early on is crucial for later adult relationships. Our experiences growing up leave a lasting imprint in our souls that determine our beliefs and expectations about how to give and receive love. These can be negative or positive depending on the family experience.

  a. Positive: a secure attachment style with that primary caregiver parent builds trust. The child feels the parent is reliable and is not afraid of abandonment. This confidence is manifested in later intimate adult relationships.

  b. Negative: There can be many negative experiences, such as divorce. Like all childhood traumas, it is important not to minimize the negative effects of this experience on the person in question. Divorce affects all the members of the family and may create issues of trust in present and future relationships. Trauma, big or small, needs to be discussed, understood, and potentially brought to counseling.[58]

---

[57] "Secure attachment" is the official term. The theory outlines what can go wrong in our early life and how our ability to love is shaped by those experiences. God designed us for connection, and it is with our parents, in family life, where this first should happen. See Milan Yerkovitch and Kay Yerkovitch, *How We Love* (Colorado Springs, CO: Waterbrook Press, 2008), 6-7.

[58] For an honest look at this subject: Wallerstein, J. S., Lewis, J., & Blakeslee, S., *The Unexpected Legacy of Divorce: A 25 Year Landmark Study*, (New York: Hyperion, 2000).

- **Circle of Friends**
  - Sounds cliche, but "birds of a feather, flock together." This refers to long-term compatibility. We hang with people who reflect a lot of who we are. Lasting marriages work better when both parties share similar values with regards to family, work, religion, etc.
  - Does he/she have "close" friends? What do they define as "close?"
  - How does he/she talk about them?
  - Do you like them? Do they seem to like you?
  - Do they have a positive or negative influence on the person in question?
  - Is he/she the same person around others as they are with you?

- **Career**
  - How did they choose this career? Why this job?
  - What motivates them?
  - Is hard work a problem for them? Do they tend to complain a lot or avoid hard work? (This could indicate a general sense of inertia/lack of motivation).

- **Money**
  - Money stress can change the dynamics of even the happiest of relationships. Stressing over finances often seeps into all other aspects of life.
  - How do each of you handle finances?

- What are your spending patterns? Look at similarities and differences. Is anyone in debt? How is he or she (or both) working on paying back loans? What is the concrete plan?

- **Friendship**
  - Friendship gives your relationship time and space to mature, allowing for boundaries to develop naturally. The simplest and most straightforward definition of a friend might be *someone who cares whether we are around or not*. A friend is a person who has a strong liking for and trust in another person. Friends love you and do not use you. Good friends help you regain trust and peace. Developing good friendships takes an investment of time and energy — something, in our quick-fix culture, we are not used to doing.
  - Friendship is key to good health and the healing of a life that has had to suffer through conflictive relationships. In a good friendship, friends desire the best for each other, requiring at times a hard dose of honesty. True friends should hold each other to higher standards and expect to call each other out when they fall short. This is not something we like, but we know we need[59]. Friendship solidifies a relationship because it is about caring about the other person's soul, not just their body.

---

[59] Good friends cannot be over-emphasized. We need people outside of our subjective world to tell us the truth objectively out of love.

Sara, 35, married, mom, Nurse

"Friendship is a necessity before there is a sexual relationship, i.e., marriage… friendship breeds trust. It is the fostering of 'this person is really there for me' and 'this person really cares for me.' The relationship is just that for now, a friendship and not sexually motivated… so, fast forward to marriage… when you can think back to the friendship that was established, there is a sense of a greater understanding that your relationship is solid and built on more than the physical. The fact that my husband and I started off as best friends gives me a greater trust in our marriage which is crucial for the times when we do let each other down and trust could even be questioned."

- **Faith**
  - One might put a question mark on this because many believe that a common faith may be important, but it is not a priority, or at least not a "deal breaker." Nonetheless, this point is not so much about *not* giving someone a chance because they do not have the same faith background. Rather, it is considering the prudent steps to take in the relationship in order to determine if that person would be someone *who can and will build me up vs bring me down.*
  - As one recent study says religion is generally a positive force in the family, at least in the United States. "Research on the connection between faith and family life shows that religion generally fosters more happiness, greater stability, and a deeper sense of meaning in American family life, provided that family members—especially spouses—share a common faith. In simple terms, the old slogan—

'the family that prays together, stays together'— still holds in 2017."[60]

- Faith values can (but not always) build people *up* because they offer important moral and spiritual standards for behavior. Some say that as long as the other is (a) searching for the truth and (b) has a moral compass with clear definitions of right and wrong, then that is enough. The question to ask is, "what *is* enough for *you*?"

- It is important to take into consideration the future-centric view, that is, the example you want to give your future children. Put simply, various research studies suggest that when it comes to faith transmission, fathers and mothers are not altogether interchangeable. According to the evidence, Fathers matter more than mothers for faith practice from adolescence to young adulthood. The data is striking.[61]

- Here are some things to think about:

  a. Long-term relationships like marriage already bring with them many potentially divisive elements that have to be worked through. These may include personal issues, health, extended family issues, career/work issues, money matters, not to mention kids in the future. Having

---

[60] Brad Wilcox, "Faith and Marriage: Better Together?", July 6, 2017, https://ifstudies.org/blog/faith-and-marriage-better-together.

[61] Formingfaith, "Dad Matters!...The Spiritual Influence of Fathers," June 18, 2015, https://formingfaith.blog/2015/06/18/dad-matters-the-spiritual-influence-of-fathers.

common faith values is just one less thing to worry about.[62]

b. Unity in a relationship is critical for building trust. Faith values underpin much of what is important in more serious decision-making because they set up a hierarchy of priorities. Unity in faith often brings with it *security and peace* in the relationship.

c. Could I see this person being the mother or father of my future children? What values do I want to see in the future mother or father of my children? Is faith one of them?

d. Am I hoping this person will grow with me in my faith journey? Do I desire that they actually challenge me to be better in my faith walk? If there aren't clear signs of a YES with this particular person, then do not proceed.

e. A "yes" to the last question means one or all of the following: a) they go to Church with me, b) they pray with me, c) they are open and interested in questions on faith, and d) they are okay hanging out with my "faith circle" of friends.[63]

f. More sticky moral issues will also come into play. One poignant way to summarize the challenges

---

[62] Wilcox, "Faith and Marriage: Better Together?".

[63] For example, as a Catholic, to see the other's willingness and commitment to continually participate in the sacraments (whether of the same or different faiths), could indicate their willingness and commitment to you and how you both desire to rear children with faith first.

of both different faiths *and* different levels of moral commitment is to ask the question: "How will you (we) react to certain real problems?" Examples include a financial calamity, a crisis within the extended family, or a special needs child.

g. Since faith values are often connected to one's political views, politics should also be discussed.

4. Conclusions of the First Two Stages of Dating

These relevant themes are fundamental to discerning if you and this person have a future. They are the building blocks of something much more than mutual attraction. Are you comfortable bringing such themes up? Why or why not? Do you find yourself discussing the relationship with others more than with your significant other? If so, ask yourself why that is, and do not be afraid to re-evaluate the relationship.

CHAPTER

Pursuing Life-Giving Relationships —
Stages Three and Four of Dating

STAGE THREE: GROWING DEEPER AS A COUPLE —
"THINGS TO LEAD WITH"

1. The first stages of romantic love are extremely motivating. We will never be as motivated to offer the best of ourselves as we are in the initial stages of dating. However, we should have some sense by now that, if we are going to really taste love, both parties need to be committed to striving for it. There is no escaping the unspoken reality of a spirit of sacrifice in this journey. The gymnasium of love *is* sacrifice. The daily grind of learning to patiently love imperfect people, despite the natural inclination to do so, is, in fact, love. It is not always pretty or picture-perfect. However, when we are courageous enough to embrace it then such love rouses the heart to new heights of love, and the impact is profound. Being accountable to one another truly brings out the best in both of you. Unfortunately, today we are bombarded with, and even succumb to, the opposite message through social media. The message is this: everything in other's relationships is just perfect. We see the carefree couple with ample amounts of disposal free time and money to travel, always having fun. Any couple with a little sense knows that this is misleading and truly inauthentic.

2. The truth of the matter is that "growing in love" means "stretching" yourself for the other. This stretching should be mutual. Are we helping each other grow or somehow hindering each other? Note: at this stage of the relationship, it is important to discuss how you resolve conflict and express sentiments of forgiveness and resentment. These are often in opposition.

- **Forgiveness**[64]
  - One of the most important dynamics in any relationship is the fine line between forgiveness and resentment. Forgiveness is the hallmark of *this love* because human beings are not perfect and will always end up hurting each other. Forgiveness is much like love. It's not a feeling, it is a choice to release the offender of the "debt" that may be owed to you. Forgiveness, like love, is a muscle that we need to exercise. If we do not use it often, it will shrivel up until rendered useless. Resentment, in turn, is the principal obstacle to forgiveness. It is a negative emotion that is common in all relationships and acts as the enemy

---

[64] Francisco Ugarte, *From Resentment to Forgiveness: A Gateway to Happiness* (Strongsville, OH: Scepter Press, 2008).

of joy. Resentment means feeling offended and not forgetting; it is a poison that produces frustration, sadness, and bitterness in the soul.

- Unless a foundation of forgiveness is cultivated, resentment will gradually infect and spread through any relationship. Based in the golden rule of love, forgiveness is the ability of one to see the humanity of the other. It says, "I too would want someone to forgive my failings." Forgiveness reminds us "you are not the arbiter of justice; rather, you are a principal of justice." We are not in control of justice in the universe. Therefore, forgiveness requires something else, *someone else*, to set the standard.

- Forgiveness is essential to any relationship and frees us from hate and resentment. It can recover the happiness that those feelings block. Forgiveness is an act of the will, not of the emotions. It is a decision. It does not eliminate the hurt but leads to an acceptance that modifies the negative feelings in a healthy way. If we don't forgive, love "cools" and can even turn into hatred, and friendship, with all its value, can be lost forever. Whether the relationship is romantic or not, forgiveness will be key to a peaceful heart.

- Some useful tools:

    a. Distinguish well between excusing and forgiving. We excuse the innocent; we forgive the guilty. It makes no sense to forgive what is excusable if the actions were involuntary: "I really didn't mean it that way." Putting yourself in the other's place often reveals how the "accused" acted out of error, distraction, or simple ignorance.

b. After forgiving the other, we can try to eliminate the negative feelings by using the wound as an occasion to feel compassion for the other, thus turning it into an incentive to pray for them.

c. Resentment can be managed if our judgment remains *objective*. This assumes the offense is neither exaggerated nor imaginary. It requires discernment and fully accounting for extenuating circumstances.

d. Gratitude perceives the goods we receive and recognizes them as gifts. If we strive to nurture a sincere spirit of gratitude in our lives, we will avoid suffering from resentment.

e. When one, in their failings, humbly recognizes their need for forgiveness, then he or she is capable of forgiving others.

f. The fundamental reason for *always* forgiving our neighbor is that God has forgiven us – and offending God through sin is infinitely more serious than any offense we can suffer.

Forgiving yourself and one another is a good gauge of maturing love. Other good gauges are attentiveness and communication. Both are vital to forming good habits of love.

- **Attentiveness to You**
  - When dating progresses to this stage, both parties need to know how the other desires to be loved. This desire is a true human need, unique to every person and not insignificant. They will need to learn to love you in that particular way, and you will need to reciprocate according to their needs. This is love.
  - Gary Chapman's book, *The Five Love Languages*, illustrates how best to communicate love.[65] These "languages" have helped many individuals and couples identify the specific way in which they desire to be shown love. The beauty of this is that the other will *show* you how they desire to be loved by what they do *for* you. An online assessment is available for free that will allow you to discover your love language. It's a very simple way of understanding who you are and what you desire in a relationship.
    a. ***Acts of Service.*** Everyone likes to be supported in the struggles of life. Making someone's life easier through doing the little things will be important for one who has this love language. Examples

---

[65] Gary Chapman, *The Five Love Languages* (Chicago: Northfield Publishing, 1995), 155-56.

include taking out the garbage, doing the dishes when visiting the other's family, pet sitting, being there for the other's family if they are going through some struggles, pitching in when needed, or running an errand. These acts of love go a long way, but consistency will be important.

b. ***Gifts.*** If you are with someone who frequently brings you little "treats" or gifts, recognize that those little things are important to them. It makes them feel loved when you give them something. It is really that simple.

c. ***Physical Touch.*** This is perhaps the easiest (as far as opportunities afford). Included are sitting around with each other on a couch touching and holding one another, bumping into one another and just hugging, holding hands when you walk, a kiss, a hug, or a touch. This is challenging for someone who does not consider themselves a "touchy-feely" type.

d. ***Words of Affirmation.*** This particular love language is really universal to all. Every human being needs and wants more affirmation in their life. The more we know how someone feels, the better it feels to be a part of their life. Sentiments expressed may include, *"I love when you share that with me," "You're amazing," "I really appreciate that," "When you do that or say that it makes me feel great."* The possibilities are endless, and we can never do it enough!

e. ***Quality Time.*** It's really important in a relationship to be present and give each other *real, non-digital* face time. Love must be more than just about *me*. It is plural; it is *other*-centered. Human beings live in relationship. Love does not just bring more than one person together; it brings people into a profound communion. This is seriously hampered when it comes to the social media age[66]. The more "human" (face to face) this can be, the better.

- **Communication**
  - A couple's ability to communicate is the single, most important contributor to a stable and satisfying long-term relationship like marriage. Let's just say that if you do not get this piece right, or at least moving in a good direction, then stop right there! Most of the serious issues with couples, dating or otherwise, can often boil down to poor communication skills. Personality differences are key to how one communicates. Some require time to process; others need to talk things out in the moment. Conflict resolution is also important. Most of us do not like conflict. Perhaps we didn't learn these skills very well growing up in our family. So, addressing and resolving conflict will not be

---

[66] It's more than just social media. It is everything from video, streaming, gaming, gambling, blogs, email, etc. This digital world is often the *antithesis* of person to person.

a skill we possess. We can be good at deflecting conflict in all kinds of unhealthy ways rather than talking it through and finding a peaceful resolution. The fact that our highly digital world does not often communicate face-to-face but rather via some other medium (phone, tablet, computer) that makes matters worse. Communication is about *who you are*. In other words, there are key personal qualities that need developing to make communication solid: a welcoming and unconditional acceptance of the other as they are, genuine honesty, and empathy.

- Doing a self and couple assessment on these points above is an excellent starting point. Remember, too, that they also need to be evaluated on an ongoing basis.

COMMUNICATION SELF-ASSESSMENT

1. This 6-question assessment should, ideally, be done 3 times: *first,* rate yourself; *second,* rate the other; *third,* let the other rate you.

2. As you consider *each* question, reflect upon it in relation to each of these three qualities, rating each on a scale of 1 to 5 (see scale next page):

a. unconditional acceptance of the other
b. genuine honesty
c. empathy

Scale:
1 = I am very poor at this behavior.
2 = I am inconsistent with this behavior.
3 = I exhibit this behavior half of the time.
4 = I am fairly consistent with this behavior.
5 = This behavior is a habit in my life.

Communication Self-Assessment Questions

1. **Is your communication clear and open?**
   a. unconditional acceptance of the other (rate 1-5)
   b. genuine honesty (rate 1-5)
   c. empathy (rate 1-5)

2. **How is well do you communicate with others (coworkers, family, friends)?**
   a. unconditional acceptance of the other (rate 1-5)
   b. genuine honesty (rate 1-5)
   c. empathy (rate 1-5)

3. **Do you talk to your family/friends/parents about the relationship more than to your significant other?**
   a. unconditional acceptance of the other (rate 1-5)
   b. genuine honesty (rate 1-5)
   c. empathy (rate 1-5)

4. **Does he/she honor you in his/her words and actions?**
   a. unconditional acceptance of the other (rate 1-5)
   b. genuine honesty (rate 1-5)
   c. empathy (rate 1-5)

5. **How well do you resolve conflict in communication?**
   a. unconditional acceptance of the other (rate 1-5)
   b. genuine honesty (rate 1-5)
   c. empathy (rate 1-5)

6. **Do you encourage one another by stating your dreams and ambitions?**
   a. unconditional acceptance of the other (rate 1-5)
   b. genuine honesty (rate 1-5)
   c. empathy (rate 1-5)

3. **Tally your results.** For a single assessment, a total of 18 or under constitutes poor communication; anything over 18 is better.

4. Most people who think they are bad communicators are usually not as bad as they think, while those who think they are good can have blind spots. In other words, there is always room for improvement.

5. **A Practical Test:** Discussing money and finance is a good, practical way to test and develop communications skills. Statistically, it may seem like money is a major cause of a failed marriage.[67] However, if you take a closer look, you will see that money matters are merely a reflection of other failing areas in the marriage. The ability to be willing to discuss money opens avenues to being open and honest all around. The best way to understand each other is to always communicate. Here are some questions to get the conversation started.

   a. What were your family's values about money growing up?

   b. Are you a "saver" or a "spender?" Why?

   c. Would an unstable income cause you extreme stress?

   d. How does each of you view debt and the paying off of debt?

   e. Do you believe the primary "breadwinner" should have the right to decide how and when the money is spent? (Take note: A future spouse who may not work outside of the house may feel differently, since he or she would be managing the household and might best know what's needed and when.)

---

[67] Nicholas Baker, "Most Common Contributing Factors to Why a Marriage Ends," https://www.familylawrights.net/blog/top-5-reasons-why-divorce-happens.

STAGE FOUR: GETTING MORE SERIOUS –
"GETTING READY TO TAKE THE NEXT STEP"

1. As the saying goes, love is "falling in love a thousand times but with the same person." At this stage of dating, there has been ample time to get to know the other person, walk through their everyday life, meet their circle of friends, and to know their family. Maturing in love can deepen and enrich appreciation in a relationship. Embracing and working through affliction can bring a special fruitfulness to the relationship. This is a good preparation for marriage which is *abundantly* filled with opportunities for purification.

2. What marks this stage is not usually the intensity of emotion or passion, however important that is[68]. Rather, the pinnacle of this stage is the *responsibility* that one feels for the other. It is this that indicates the true measure of their love.

   • Am I willing to make sacrifices for the other in very specific ways, putting my needs and wants aside for what he or she may need?
   • Is the other willing to do the same for me, or is it always a one-sided deal?
   • Is the other actively finding out how to love me better?

---

[68] It is important to note the opposite reality, too, which is where very little emotion is felt. Just because you don't feel like you are in love, doesn't mean you don't have the capacity or ability to love.

3. In the beginning, when everything is new, there are few obstacles to enjoying each other's presence. Yet, as time goes on, and because we are all flawed human beings, the "cracks in the armor" begin to appear in our character. Some of these human deficiencies might be due to ignorance or lack of forming of good habits, while others are more innate. In other words, some can be overcome with a little more personal effort, while others are just the way the person is and thus are unlikely ever going to change.

4. It is at this point that couples may consider doing an *inventory*. See the Appendix for a listing of couple inventories that allow couples to identify areas of their relationships that need work and maturity. This booklet advocates doing some form of an inventory earlier rather than later, such as before one is engaged, to discover irreconcilable differences. The "gut check" below is a simple form of the same.

THE "GUT CHECK"

Each party must decide how important these "cracks" are to the relationship. Remember dating is *not* recreational. It is about the evaluation of a very important decision. It challenges us to a deeper reflection over mere reaction. It is also a mistake to think that God is not interested in our good or bad choices. He desires our happiness. Prayerful conversation with Him will also be vital for your own peace of mind and in deciding to move forward or not.

- Are you honest about recognizing the weaknesses of yourself and the other?
- Do you see what they shared about themselves as matching up with how they act? In other words, is there a level of coherent honesty in their behavior with strangers, family, and friends?
- Have you noticed any patterns of dishonesty? Has anyone close to you mentioned their concerns about any character traits that they see?
- Are you interested in the person that he or she is right now or *the potential* this person has, what they could be if this or that changed?
- Evaluate if you are truly happy with how he or she is *today*. If this person did not change in the next 10 years, would you still marry them?[69]

A CRITICAL QUESTION THAT YOU NEED TO ASK AND ANSWER

Is that particular thing that you have witnessed in the other something that **you simply could not live with** (if it didn't change)? If the answer is, in all honesty, "YES" then the next questions is:

- Have you spoken about it directly with the person?
- If NO, then you need to do so because this *is a gamechanger* for the relationship, particularly if the relationship is more advanced.

---

[69] This is a HUGE question to ponder.

- If YES, and this particular thing has not changed over a reasonable period of time, then better to decide now to end the relationship.

SOME POSSIBLE WARNING SIGNS

- **The Moody, Won't Talk Type.** If a couple can't talk to each other, their future is dim. Beware of the person who retreats into their shell, who is unable to share what is on their mind, the sulker, the pouter, the one who stonewalls with silence rather than discussing their grief in a reasonable manner. Of course, we all have moments of moodiness, but the person who seems to do this habitually will be the most difficult to communicate with in the future on a variety of important subjects.
- **Emotionally Extreme Type.** All of us have moments where we "blow up" or can be over-the-top with excitement or overwhelmed with sadness. Yet, some mastery of our emotional world is critical for clear thinking and teamwork in any relationship. Those who are easily triggered to anger, ready for a fight at the slightest imagined insult, are not going to be easy to deal with. So, too, is the person who is so touchy

that they shut down or explode at any suggestion of criticism. Extreme reactions such as too much self-pity, jealousy or envy fall into the same category.

- **A Conflictive Value System.** Experience shows healthy and strong marriages tend to be based on a common view of life and on commitment. If there are fundamental values that are not in alignment in your relationship, or even clash with each other (i.e., faith, morality, prospect of children and how to raise them), this is a recipe for later disaster.

- **The Drinker.** Disordered alcohol use is more common than you may imagine. Studies have revealed that 29.1 percent of the US population has experienced an alcohol use disorder (of varying grades) at some point in their lifetime.[70] If the person in question has an issue, like pornography, most likely they will be in denial. Almost every alcoholic at one time was sure that "it could never happen to them."

- **Unhealthy Family Dynamics.** It is true that you will marry a man or a woman and not the whole family, but you may be surprised at the part in-laws (and in-law siblings) play in the lives of many married couples. Certain behavioral dependencies on the parents or siblings may spell trouble for building a unified, trustful relationship. Generally speaking, any person that appears to interfere with a particular family dynamic

---

[70] "Alcoholism: Symptoms and Signs," American Addiction Centers, Feb 3, 2020, https://americanaddictioncenters.org/alcoholism-treatment/symptoms-and-signs.

can become an unconscious "enemy" of the parent. One typical expression of this is when the person you are dating is slow to defend you from the criticism of one or both parents. In other words, they seem to stay neutral to keep the peace or are not willing to stand up to their parents or siblings.

- **Persons Who Lack Responsibility.** Everybody has to shoulder responsibility. If one has a problem with learning to accept obligations when they are single, it will also be a problem when they are married. So, the irresponsible young man at twenty-five is not likely to be a rock of responsibility at thirty-five.

- **The Problem of Narcissism.** A strong streak of selfishness makes people incapable of looking beyond themselves, beyond their own desires and needs. Each sex manifests narcissistic behavior in a different way *and* at the expense of the other. "Men are likely to emphasize intellect, power, aggression, money, or social status. Women are likely to emphasize body, looks, charm, sexuality, feminine "traits", homemaking, children, and childrearing."[71] This can easily translate into certain behaviors. For a man, it looks like go and dominate, control, conquer, and take what others will give you in business or in love. For women, it looks like doing anything to feel loved, secure, noticed, and desired, and do whatever is necessary to keep this feeling of love.

---

[71] Sam Vaknin, "Gender and the Narcissist - Female Narcissist," November 16, 2008, https://www.healthyplace.com/personality-disorders/malignant-self-love/gender-and-the-narcissist.

- **Objectification.** Our materialistic society has also pushed these negative attitudes onto human love. Persons are disposable. "We treat affective relationships the way we treat material objects and the environment: everything is disposable; everyone uses and throws away, takes and breaks, exploits and squeezes to the last drop. Then, goodbye."[72] Perceived self-worth is therefore often based on material and social factors. Lifelong fidelity to one person is seen as not possible or even desired. "There are too many headaches to be with the same person all your life." "We can always start all over again" when love becomes not fun. "It is the culture of the ephemeral…the speed with which people move from one affective relationship to another. They believe, along the lines of social networks, that love can be connected or disconnected at the whim of the consumer, and the relationship quickly 'blocked'."[73]

Martin Connor, LC, Priest, Author of *Reclaiming Love*

"Authentic love is most perfectly expressed through the public promises one makes when committing to the state of marriage. The fullness of human love is not compatible with 'trial' marriages or commitments. Rather, it demands a surrender, a total and definitive gift of a person to another… through making a free choice to publicly commit to marriage, rather than being somehow limited or weakened by the act, the person is actually enriched and made more perfect."

---

[72] Pope Francis, *The Joy of Love: Post-Synodal Apostolic Exhortation, Amortis Laetitia, of the Holy Father Francis to Bishops, Priests and Deacons, Consecrated Persons, Christian Married Couples and All the Lay Faithful on Love in the Family,* 39.

[73] Ibid.

CHAPTER

Pursuing Life-Giving Relationships — Stage Five of Dating

1. How long should you date? To this thousand-dollar question, consider this. First, though happiness is a desire we all have, we also know that it is not guaranteed all the time in this life. Marriage brings happiness and sadness in one's life. Be *very* careful on centering your desires solely on the question "will this person make me happy?" Rather, look long term, the end game, beyond this life to heaven. There is only one sensible answer to the question: "How long should one really date?" As long as necessary to make you reasonably sure that this person can or cannot help you fulfill the most vital task in life: getting to heaven! If you decide yes, you are ready for the altar. If you decide no, you should break off the relationship. The key word here

is ***reasonably***. What is important is that the infatuation phase, so often seen in the early stages of dating, needs to pass as you enter into the more serious stages of dating.

2. To go beyond the infatuation phase, it is helpful to ask yourself the following questions before you think about engagement:

- Will this person help me fulfill my most vital task in life, getting to heaven?[74]
- Will this person be a good father or mother to our children?
- Does this person give me a reasonable assurance of long-term fidelity "until death do us part?"

3. It is also important to make sure you are making this decision in serenity and freedom. The middle of a stressful career change or personal trauma, financial difficulties, or an unplanned pregnancy, etc. should never be catalysts for rushing the most important decision of your life.

4. It is doubtful that one can be certain about such an important thing if you've only known someone for a few months. Yet, on the other hand, you can be too discerning in wanting to be absolutely certain (impossible!) or wanting everything to be perfectly "in place" before taking the step (unrealistic!).

---

[74] Whether you are a believer or not, this is a worthy question? Begin with the end in mind: What is the ultimate purpose of my life?

5. Lastly, while there are some wedding traditions that go in and out of style, there's one that never will: asking your future wife's parents for their blessing. A recent study revealed that 70% of all engagements happen with the partner's dad and/or mom's loving approval, a tradition that became popular in the 18th century.[75] This tradition, in particular, is a request to transition the woman from her father's (or parents) responsibility to her future husband's. This has nothing to do with a rejection of feminism. Rather, it is simply honoring a tradition that is a healthy gesture of respect. Still, a prospective groom would be wise to check in with his fiancé before approaching her parents in case there are possible conflicts. Even if it's not your cup of tea, but you know it would mean a lot to your beloved and her parents, it's a sweet, courteous and respectful thing to do.[76]

SHORT OR LONG ENGAGEMENT?

1. First, remember that *engagement does not equal marriage*. You can break off the engagement at any moment, if over time, you realize a true incompatibility.

---

[75] Lindsay Goldenberg Jones, "The Right Way to Ask a Dad to Marry His Daughter," April 7, 2017, https://www.womangettingmarried. com/how-to-ask-a-dad-to-marry-his-daughter.

[76] Any father of girls knows deep down that he is ultimately responsible for protecting his daughter's virtue. When she marries, her *husband* becomes responsible for protecting her virtue. So, before marrying, it's important to respect the father's authority before moving forward.

2. The truth is that becoming engaged is the beginning of a very serious stage in your life. In fact, it is one of the most serious stages you will engage in your lifetime. By the time you arrive at this part of the booklet you are probably getting this point. Investment in a possible long-term relationship like marriage is not a small thing. It is demanding and quite serious.

3. If you in good conscience have embraced growing together and done much of what was suggested in the earlier part of this book, then a shorter engagement is not high risk. What *is* fundamental before you marry is that sufficient time is given so that each person can truly discover and know the other: convictions, dreams, values, motivations. Questions of "compatibility" are for the dating stages. Engagement is a time to go deeper, a time for more challenging discussions about the application of those first discussions. For example, dating - what is your view of x, y, and z? Engaged - how can we work together to ensure x, y, and z grows and flourishes, so we are building a solid foundation for our marriage and family?

4. Longer engagements have their undesirable aspects too. Are the reasons to delay your marriage reasonable or simply convenient? Those reasons need to be weighed very seriously. Once you know you want to spend your life with this person and you want to have a family with them, why delay?

5. Once engaged, it is important to confidently communicate to your family and wedding party that your wedding is truly a sacred occasion and not just one more "dance and drink" party. This is not to be underestimated. Aligning expectations for your wedding day with those most involved adds a much-needed measure of seriousness and can avoid the typical shallowness and superficiality that often appear on such occasions. While a wedding is an absolutely joyful occasion, you may just want to make sure that the sacredness is not lost in the festivity of the reception.

6. Based on a one-year timeline, for example, the engagement period can be divided into three important phases:

- **Period One:** Initial announcement and "okay, what do we need to do?"
- **Period Two:** Let's persevere and prepare well.
- **Period Three:** The imminent celebration.

PERIOD ONE: INITIAL ANNOUNCEMENT AND "OKAY, WHAT DO WE NEED TO DO?"

If you find yourself engaged and you have just come upon this little booklet, here are some best practices to consider if you want to prepare well for your wedding day (beyond just the invitation list and reception).

- **Make a Plan.** In many respects, the real work is just beginning. Now you *are* getting married! The words were spoken, "Will you marry me?" and the answer was "Yes." Once you both get beyond the excitement of the announcement, it is time to sit down and make a plan.
- **Choose a Date.** Calendars out, schedules reviewed. This will also depend on the physical place in which you choose to be married. **Attention! Many churches require more time to reserve dates.**
- **Who Will Officiate the Ceremony?** Usually, but not always, the officiant is the same person that helps the couple prepare for marriage. If it is a religious ceremony, the formal preparation will depend on each Church leader and the pathway they suggest.
- **Get a Mentor.** It is a good idea to consider formal or informal meetings with mature married couples. Sometimes this is already set up by your Church or community. Consider any couple in your family or social circles that have been a great example of marital joy and consistency. This is a good place to start in reflecting on what is ahead for both of you.
- **Find Resources to Help You.** Online questionnaires and other materials are available in abundance and help greatly prepare a couple for marriage. (See Chapter XI for Resources).
- **Engage in Spiritual Preparation.** Consider doing a spiritual retreat individually to prepare. Some prefer

to do a weekend couples retreat which is a good opportunity to get away, to be with other couples, and to discuss the foundational principles of building a good marriage with other couples.

PERIOD TWO: "LET'S PERSEVERE AND PREPARE WELL"

1. **Go Deeper in Conversation.** Once the ring is "on the finger" and the commitment has been made, then discussions of certain topics such as, finances, family of origin, sexual intimacy, and babies, will have a different tone. This new level of commitment to marriage sheds light on issues you talked about before, but now this decision actually allows you to go much deeper. Here are some questions that might reflect the *depth* of conversation that engagement affords:

- Do you share the same vision of what marriage is and what it entails?
- Do you share the same long-term goals and dreams?
- Would it be helpful to craft a motto or mission statement about where you see yourselves as a couple, identifying priorities, virtues, and goals you will pursue?

- Can you see yourself waking up next to this person for the rest of your life?
- Can you picture yourself saying "I love you" to your future spouse when you are on your last straw with him or her?
- Can you come to terms with putting your future spouse before yourself in daily activities for the rest of your life?
- Discuss general parenting and children desires. Can you see that your future spouse will be a good and loving parent?
- Discuss in more detail how money will be managed and spent. Will one person administer? Both? Will you have one, joint account or individual accounts or both? Craft a budget and decide what your spending priorities will be.
- Are there aspects of your fiancé's temperament or behavior that you find hurtful, and have you spoken with them about this? Are you prepared to grow and correct aspects of your temperament or behavior that are incompatible with loving your future spouse completely?
- Hurts from the past may surface from deeper reflection and self-examination. Honest reconciliation[77] with yourself, your fiancé, and with God are important. In doing so, you will have the freedom to bring one

---

[77] For Catholics, it is recommended to go to the sacrament of reconciliation before marrying. In fact, a thorough confession of your entire life allows the weight of past mistakes to be given to God and peace will reign as He blesses your life in marriage.

chapter of your life to a close and to open a brand new one with great expectation and hope.

2. **Personalize Your Rules as a Couple.** Studies show that all people seem to have "unspoken rules,"[78] but they are rarely expressed until they are broken by someone else. By identifying what some of those hidden rules might be, you both avoid unnecessary explosions. Laying down common ground rules for your own marriage is something you can mutually commit to and develop together. Some examples:

- Not sharing intimate topics about your relationship with outsiders.
- Not criticizing in-laws to others.
- Never raising your voice.
- Keeping a policy of honest communication (the more detailed, the better).
- Not going to sleep angry at the other.
- Always paying the bills punctually.
- Cleaning habits, socializing, punctuality.

3. **Create an Invitation List.** Conversations about such substantial topics also helps with determining who is invited to the wedding. This is not just another party. You are inviting people to witness your commitment. This type of discernment helps turn the invitation list from a simple action item to a meaningful process.

---

[78] See the excellent resource: Les Parrott and Leslie Parrott, *Saving Your Marriage Before It Starts* (Grand Rapids: Zondervan, 2006), 22-24.

4. Begin the Wedding Preparation.

- The announcement of a wedding is probably one of the most joyous human occasions in life. It can be a very blessed time of celebration for families; a time to come together and rally around each other. It can also be, in some cases, a catalyst for healing relationships. This happens when the preparation is done with a spirit of love and the family feels included. It is also the "first project" you both get to work on together, and it is a time of building intimacy for both parties. It can be a good reflection of what married life will look like.

- The engagement period is also a great time to strengthen your relationship with your in-laws. It has been said that on your wedding night you arrive with two suitcases: one with your clothes, one with your family history (or "junk"). It is true you are not marrying the parents. On the other hand, this person whom you love is extremely important to their parents and family and, therefore, they should be important to you, too.

- Don't shy away from the pageantry of a wedding. This is designed to be set apart from the rest, to underscore the importance and sacredness of the day. Plan the toasts and speeches for the reception well and give those involved sufficient time to prepare. This is an important moment allowing family members and friends to express their love and enrich the moment.

- The biggest risk of the engagement period is to lose focus on the adventure you are beginning because you are so focused on the wedding day. Wedding preparation can be very stressful. Also, everyone wants to give their opinion. It can be financially stressful as well. You may forget what happens after the wedding day. Don't let that happen.

5. **Keep a Keen Eye on Finances.**[79] Be cognizant of this fact: There is an entire industry built around expensive weddings. Be careful about falling into the "keeping up with the Jones'" mentality. There are other ways of celebrating the beginning of your married life that do not involve a heavy financial investment. Some examples:

- Some couples decide to keep everything simple and give the money to the less fortunate.
- Cutting corners does not necessarily mean being "cheap." Couples can opt to have certain details covered in ways that are not as expensive (the venue, the table arrangements, and the flowers). Within every family there are talented people, and most are quite happy to contribute to making the celebration special *and* more cost-effective.

---

[79] General wisdom about money in marriage: "share everything." Both parties should have access to everything. This doesn't mean both will necessarily utilize the same accounts, but both should be able to access all of the money because, as a married couple, it belongs to BOTH of you.

6. **The Marriage Ceremony: Before, During, and After.**
   Generally, people arrive at a wedding celebration with a positive and open spirit. It is the perfect to impact friends and family with the truth through the joy and beauty of your commitment. The ceremony itself is the center of your wedding day, the time when you make a vow of perpetual love to the other. Take the time necessary to plan it well. Ask for advice from people who know. For example, the Catholic Church offers engaged couples many creative ways to personalize their wedding ceremony. There are some powerful things you can do during the ceremony in collaboration with your pastor. For example:

   - Writing letters to each other with the pastor reading them during the ceremony as part of the sermon.
   - Washing the feet of your spouse (usually at the beginning of the reception).

7. **The Honeymoon.** There is no question that a honeymoon is an important way to celebrate joyfully the beginning of a new chapter of your life. It is a necessary "high point," free from the concerns of the world, and exclusively focused on the person you love.

PERIOD THREE: "THE IMMINENT CELEBRATION"

1. The last months or weeks leading up to the wedding are generally stressful. Details, Details, Details. Remember, it is the wedding celebration that is the culmination of your love and commitment and not the details related to everything else. So, what keeps you united in the madness? Remembering the "why!" If you have invested in the necessary time in preparing yourselves and now freely embrace what you are about to commit to, then this preparation is exactly what gives you interior peace, "all will be well" despite any conflicts that may arise.

2. Some vital things to remember in this unique moment of your life:

   • Make your wedding day a new beginning in your relationship with your spouse: forgive one another, reconcile with God, look to the future and not the past.
   • It is a mentally healthy thing to do to try to set aside all that it took to get there and enjoy the blessed moment that is upon you, surrounded by everyone you love.
   • It's important to confidently communicate your desires to make this moment as special as possible. Make sure your family, and more importantly, the members of the wedding party understand this. This is truly a sacred occasion and not just one more "dance and drink" party. Aligning expectations for your wedding day with those most involved adds a much-needed measure of

seriousness to the event. Doing so can help you avoid the typical shallowness and superficiality that often appears on such occasions.

3. During the Ceremony

- Be yourself! Don't give in to the "temptations" of the world that have more to do with your guests' partying and less with your love and commitment to one another.
- Keep focused on the vows.
- Pray for each other.

10

Living Together –
The Statistics Say the Opposite[80]

Colton Dixon, American Idol alum, newly married to Annie Coggeshall

"It was not easy!... But I believe sex was designed for marriage and I knew it would be more meaningful to wait. That was something I grew up thinking and feeling... [once married] There were a lot of moments of – 'Oh, you're not going back to your room. That means we're married!' It made it really special for us."

Annie

"It wasn't because someone was telling me this is what you should do. Deep down in my heart it felt like it was the right thing. And we're really glad we did. We know God's hand is on our marriage."

---

1. Cohabitation is an arrangement where two people are not married but live together. They are often, but not always,

---

80 Connor LC, *Reclaiming Love*, 47-48.

involved in a romantic or sexually intimate relationship on a long-term or permanent basis. Such arrangements have become increasingly common in Western countries since the late 20th century, being led by changing social views especially regarding marriage, gender roles, and religion. A high percentage of people today cohabitate outside of marriage. It is now normative behavior.

2. The Christian view has always advocated waiting for marriage before engaging in sexual relations. It is special and it is sacred. Sexual relations are for bonding and for babies. By separating these two realities, the beauty of the experience has been cheapened and degraded. Sexual intercourse is God's "design system" to bring lots of people into the world, forming families which are the necessary building blocks for a healthy and happy society. The increased number of couples living together has not seemed to increase the happiness in the world.[81] It may seem intuitive, and even prudent, that two people should live together before making the very serious and lifelong commitment of marriage. Living together to discover if, in fact, they are "really" compatible makes sense, right?

3. However, *the statistics say the opposite.* A summary of research shows that "the expectation of a positive relationship between cohabitation and marital stability...

---

[81] Laura DeRose, "Cohabitation, Marriage, and the Happiness Gap," November 4, 2019, https://ifstudies.org/blog/cohabitation-marriage-and-the-happiness-gap.

has been shattered in recent years by studies conducted in several Western countries."[82] What the studies discovered is this: if you do not want to get divorced, do not move in together until after the wedding.

4. What were some of the other facts found? Most couples who live together never end up getting married, but those who do tie the knot have a divorce rate nearly 80 percent higher than those who waited until after the wedding to move in together.[83] Couples who live together prior to marriage also have greater marital conflict and poorer communication, and they made more frequent visits to marriage counselors.[84] Women who live with their boyfriends were also more than three times as likely to be depressed as married women,[85] and the couples were less sexually satisfied than those who waited for marriage.[86]

---

[82] William G. Axinn and Arland Thornton, "The Relation Between Cohabitation and Divorce: Selectivity or Causal Influence?" *Demography*, 29:3 (August 1992), 357-374.

[83] Neil G. Bennett, Ann Klimas Blanc, and David E. Bloom, "Commitment and the Modern Union: Assessing the Link Between Premarital Cohabitation and Subsequent Marriage Stability," *American Sociological Review*, 53:1 (February 1988), 127-138.

[84] Elizabeth Thompson and Ugo Colella, "Cohabitation and Marital Stability: Quality or Commitment?", *Journal of Marriage and the Family*, 54 (1992), 263; John D. Cunningham and John K. Antill, "Cohabitation and Marriage: Retrospective and Predictive Consequences," *Journal of Social and Personal Relationships*, 11 (1994), 90.

[85] Lee Robins and Darrell Regier, *Psychiatric Disorders in America: The Epidemiologic Catchment Area Study* (New York: Free Press, 1991), 64.

[86] Marianne K. Hering, "Believe Well, Live Well," Focus on the Family, September 1994, 4.

THE BEDROCK OF TRUST

1. Deeper reasons point to the fact that living together does not begin with the bedrock of *trust* as marriage does; rather, it begins with a certain suspicion that "we may not be right for each other, so let's test this." Two individuals *hope* they might "be right for each other" but suspect it is a real possibility they may not be, for any number of reasons. This is a different mindset from the couple who knows that there will be challenges, yet their common commitment to a higher ideal of permanency in marriage, aided by God's grace and the community, assures them they *can* be faithful. The institution of marriage expresses just this: you vow publicly before each other and the community, *trusting* that with the help of God and your community, both persons will persevere "till death do us part." When a couple commits to this ideal publicly before those who are most vested in helping them, statistics support that this is of huge benefit to the couple and to the entire human community.[87]

2. Dr. Edward Sri, from the Augustine Institute in Denver, explains well this reality of unrequited love in living together:

---

[87] Brian Hollar, "Regular Church Attenders Marry more, Divorce Less Than Their Less Devout Peers," March 4, 2020, https://ifstudies.org/blog/regular-church-attenders-marry-more-and-divorce-less-than-their-less-devout-peers.

"Sexual intimacy outside of marriage can create an impression of a closeness that does not really exist between people. In their bodies they say, 'I'm totally yours.' But in reality, their hearts merely say, 'I'm yours… until someone better comes around.' In such a relationship, the other person is not truly committed to you as a person. They are more committed to the sensual pleasure and emotion they derive from you. And they could just as easily get their sexual and emotional needs met from someone else down the road. The lack of committed love breeds fear and insecurity".[88]

3. Yet, "shotgun cohabitations" are quickly overtaking "shotgun marriages." Living together before marriage is often called a commitment to a non-commitment. Most couples seem to "slide" into living together rather than make a clear decision about what it means and what their futures may hold. One person lives the commitment in a way that is all-in, almost as if they were in a marital state, while the other continues to live as if they were just "roommates." One party sadly, very often the female, enters into a new stage of the relationship with different expectations than the other party. Seeking stability and security in her life, she perhaps thinks, "If I live with him, this is the right next step to marriage." Meanwhile, he is thinking, "Sure I care about her and maybe we can make

---

[88] Edward Sri, *Unveiled Love* (San Francisco: Ignatius Press, 2015), 252-253.

this work, but I am good the way we are right now." Other than trying to be aware of and caring for the others needs at a basic level, nothing really changes for him. As one young woman reflected, "It was like we were both caring for the same person – him. I felt left out of it."[89]

4. Once the rationalizing of the other's behavior and the fear of drawing the line sets in (because that would be the real test of love), mutual benefit breaks down and mistrust enters. As one girl said, "If you have to give a guy something sexual to keep him, you are going to lose him anyway, because he doesn't really love you."[90] A former "playboy" put it this way in his blog, "Look, talk is cheap. Ladies listen, guys are good salesman, they can tell you they love you and they might even mean it when they say it, but if they will wait until your wedding night to have sex with you, they probably mean it."[91]

5. In a scenario of living together, a continual litany of unanswered questions will abound: "How much can I really hope to experience the total love I long for in this concrete situation?" "Can I entrust myself to this person, as I truly am, and yet not receive the same in return?" "How can this relationship bring me the future happiness that I

---

[89] Chrystilina Evert, *Pure Womanhood* (Scottsdale, AZ: Totus Tuus Press, 2018), 17.

[90] Evert, *Pure Womanhood*, 19.

[91] Rob Kowolski, "10 Reasons Why Not to Have Sex Before Marriage", June 6, 2017, https://medium.com/@robbkowalski/10-reasons-not-to-have-sex-before-marriage-7c6c85964be7.

desire?" This type of questioning breeds distrust because you are constantly second guessing the other's intentions.

Marie, 28, single, Consultant

"Strongest argument not to have sex before marriage? Well, the older I get, the biggest one for me is understanding that my body and soul are worth not being used by someone else."

---

6. "As the increasingly popular romantic path for young adults today: date, cohabit a while, then (maybe) get married becomes more commonplace, the lines between getting married and just moving in together can begin to blur. This will make it harder for young people to recognize what is so special about the marriage vows. But despite prevailing myths about cohabitation being similar to marriage, research is showing that when it comes to the relationship quality measures that count—like commitment, satisfaction, and stability—research continues to show that marriage is still the best choice for a strong and stable union."[92] It also shows that living together has greatly increased in large measure because, while people are delaying marriage to ever greater ages, they are not delaying sex or childbearing.[93] These facts come with their own risks.

---

[92] Brad Wilcox, "Cohabitation Doesn't Compare: Marriage, Cohabitation, and Marriage Quality," February 7, 2019, https://ifstudies.org/blog/cohabitation-doesnt-compare-marriage-cohabitation-and-relationship-quality.

[93] Scott Stanley, "Cohabitation is Pervasive," June 20, 2018, https://ifstudies.org/blog/cohabitation-is-pervasive.

SOME TYPICAL ISSUES THAT COME WITH PRE-MARITAL SEX

1. **Sex Masks Problems.** It is easy to think that sex can resolve problems. It delays, or worse, buries dealing with the real problems in the relationship.

2. **Sex Connects.** Our very biology says sex is a mechanism hardwired into us to help bond us, to connect us, *for the long-term*. Why? Sexual intercourse brings babies into the world who need a stable and secure home of love. Yet pre-marital sex is so often reduced to something *recreational*. We like fun without the responsibility. This is not part of God's plan. He wired us for love and to safeguard the next generation. His plan is centered on communicating something eternal. This is why lovers do not see their love as merely temporary. Love expressed through the one flesh union is about babies and bonding together; the wedding vows say this publicly. The vows are renewed when male and female come together in the sexual act itself and say "I love you now *and* forever."[94] Those who marry do not expect their excitement to fade. This is where biology and theology meet.

3. **Sex is Instant Gratification.** Sex never produces long-term happiness. Not in one single thing. Sex seems to produce instant happiness, but there's a price to be paid

---

[94] The spousal meaning of the body is the ability of the human body, in its masculinity or femininity, to express and realize our call to a communion of persons through self-giving love.

for this down the road. Love, expressed in sexual intimacy as a total gift of self to another, communicates a desire to love forever and not just for one instant or one more superficial moment in the life of a person.

4. **Sex is About Bonding and Babies.** Couples who are engaging in regular sex should know that babies are not a "mistake," something actually went right! In the case of the increasing rate of people living together, they are more likely to have children together, less likely to eventually marry, and more likely to "serial cohabitate."[95] Therefore, children born to cohabiting parents face a significant risk of instability throughout their life as they cope with their parents' relationship transitions. The child's education and health are affected, and there is a significant increase in risk of abuse and poverty.

BE GOOD TO YOURSELF, GET THE FACTS, WEIGH YOUR CHOICES

Here is a summary of reasons to postpone sexual activity until in a committed state, like marriage:

- Gives true dignity to you and your significant other.
- True sexual freedom exists only when the dignity of the human person is recognized.
- A true sense of security: STD's and pregnancy are eliminated as a possibility.

---

[95] "Effects of Cohabitation on Children," Marripedia, http://marripedia.org/effects_of_cohabitation_on_children.

- Ultimate control over your own body.
- Allows opportunity to invest *in the person* and to know if they are the one to marry.
- Allows you to clearly evaluate the quality of current and future relationships.
- Protects your fertility from damaging and life-threatening STD's and birth control.
- Allows the development of true intimacy which is friendship being at the center of a relationship.
- Differences and weaknesses of others are thoroughly explored and discovered.
- Statistically far less likely to divorce.
- You will know that your significant other is truly appreciating *you* instead of just being available.
- Allows clear thinking for personal goals.

WHY MUST I WAIT WHEN I CAN HAVE IT RIGHT NOW?

1. If doing whatever you like without any real mature reflection is the way to go, then why are so many unhappy? It takes much effort in the ambit of love to make the right choices. There is that constant voice inside us, and all around us, that blares the message "go for it," regardless of consequences. Today, the only way to express love is through sexual intimacy, right? It seems as though the measurement of "love" in a relationship is often linked to the frequency of sex. Of course, this is not true, but we can be made to believe this

Yet, there are other ways to express love.

2. Abstinence, for example, is a free choice to abstain from sexual intimacy while expressing love. Besides protecting one from sexually transmitted infections, the benefits are many. They have nothing to do with religion; they are actually part of our design as human beings. Part of our design is that when we distance ourselves from something we like, it makes us want it more. Relate that to food, drink, and sex. When you take a break from something, you grow in appreciation for it. Take for example chocolate cake. If you ate it every day or even the entire thing in one sitting, you would lose the desire for it and probably get sick. This is a disordered approach to eating cake. Cake can be good and savored when ordered properly such as to celebrate a special occasion. Abstinence follows the same rule. Waiting builds the desire and suspense for the experience. When you keep the distraction of sexual interaction out of your dating relationship, it allows you to develop a friendship, learn about who each of you really is, what is going to work and what is not going to work. As you grow in love, and once you are married, you will always have this friendship to rely on as the foundation of your relationship.

3. Sacrifice out of love for another makes us better. Chaste dating is all about one thing: delaying gratification. Self-control, not just for love but for any reason, has never been easy for people. Today self-control is definitely not

very common. Yet, the greatest success stories in human history are about human beings ***putting the goal first before themselves***. The goal of dating is marriage, to find that soulmate with whom you can build a life together based on authentic, mutual love. Marriages are proven to be more fulfilling and last longer when people respect one another in all things. Marriage is the truest form of that gift of self in love because one chooses to save that *total* gift for the person they marry.

CHAPTER 11

Final Exhortation and Recommended Resources

1. What is the essence of being human? Loving. Without it we cannot be fulfilled nor be happy. Robots can't love. Red roses can't love. *We can love*.

2. Dating is a necessary training ground for growing in our capacity for authentic love till we find that soulmate. That's right, ***grow***! If you are ready to give and give for the rest of your life, then you are ready to date. Even the reality of breaking up does not disqualify the important fact that we DID grow, we did learn, we did love. The habits, emotional maturity, and even material possessions ((trinkets, jewelry, memorabilia from travel, photos, etc.) accumulated from past relationships continue to serve you well in your life. They have added value to your life that you carry with you as you create new memories from your experiences in new places, enriched by new relationships with amazing people.

3. Dating reminds us that, while we cannot control other people, we do have a say in the way we live our lives and the kind of people we become. All relationships are an opportunity to look challenges in the eye and come out a stronger person.

IS MARRIAGE THE ONLY PATH TO HAPPINESS?

1. Let us be perfectly clear to all those who might think marriage is the surest path to happiness. Marriage *can* bring happiness but not perfect happiness. Marriage is certainly not the only path to happiness. Heartfelt yearning for perfect love may be awakened by a relationship with another person, but no one can completely or perfectly satisfy this yearning. It is a desire for fullness that is *out of proportion* with our human capacity to quench it for the other. Why? Because that desire is of divine origin. God made us for himself; it is his way of drawing us to himself.

2. "The desire for God is written in the human heart, because man is created by God and for God... Only in God will he find the truth and happiness he never stops searching for".[96] Therefore, only the perfect love of God can truly fulfill this deep desire.

3. It would be wrong of us not to mention that some people are not called to marriage as we know it in this life. They are called to live in the world and be a sign here on earth of the eternal marriage in heaven. The God of revelation

---

[96] *CCC*, 27.

does call some men and women to complete chastity, radical poverty, and a new obedience, all for the sake of the kingdom of heaven.[97]

4. Such a decision does not extinguish one's sexuality. It does not suffocate, set aside, or forget all the beautiful masculine or feminine gifts. Rather, a celibate dedication to love is the redirection of an energy from its immediate goal to a higher spiritual or social aim[98] It is a calling to re-channel all those human gifts to a noble and beautiful purpose—leading others to heaven!

5. This is essentially what priests and other consecrated men and women represent. They have encountered that perfect love and now live exclusively for that love in this life. Those who are called to this pathway say to us with their example, "Set your eyes on the truth of that perfect love!"

6. What about those who are not called either to marriage, priesthood, or consecrated life? Or those who believe that are called to marriage yet have not found a spouse? Does a single person have a call to love? Yes! "All Christians in any state or walk of life are called to the fullness of Christian life and to the perfection of love."[99].

---

[97] Thomas Dubay, *And You are Christ's* (San Francisco: Ignatius Press, 1987), 24.

[98] Dubay, *And You are Christ's*, 28.

[99] *CCC*, 2013.

RECOMMENDED RESOURCES

Personal development resources are abundantly available today. Human flourishing takes place when the body *and* soul are growing, not one without the other. Throughout the entire booklet, the need for more personal introspection through self and couple assessment has been emphasized. The following resources are meant to help you find solid food for the head *and* the heart so as to grow in authentic love. Remember, this is the bedrock of healthy dating.

1. **Podcasts**
   - Among the Lilies (women)
   - Do Something Beautiful (women)
   - Fiat 90 (women)
   - The Catholic Gentleman (men)
   - Exodus 90 (men)
   - Lust is Boring, Jason Evert (all)
   - UMD Newman Catholic (all)
   - The Place We Find Ourselves (all)
   - Ask Christopher West (all)
   - Catholic Late Night (all)

2. **YouTube Channels**
   - Emily Wilson
   - Overt TV
   - Matt Fradd
   - Ascension Presents

- The Inversion of Masculine and Feminine in Popular Culture.
- Sisters of Life.

3. Websites
- CatholicYenta.com
- FamilyHonor.org
- CatholicChemistry.com
- OFWCMedia.com
- DumbOxMinistries.com
- LovedAlready.com
- TheRadianceFoundation.org

4. Books on Dating, Sexuality, Gender
- *Emotional Virtue*, Sarah Swafford
- *Reclaiming Love*, Martin Connor LC
- *Wild at Heart*, John Eldredge
- *Captivating*, John and Stasi Eldredge
- *How to Find Your Soulmate Without Losing Your Soul,* Jason and Crystallina Evert
- *The Porn Myth,* Matt Fradd
- *Delivered*, Matt Fradd
- *Uncompromising Purity*, Kelsey Skoch

5. Dating After Divorce
- Dating After Divorce: vimeo.com/123306508
- VinceFrese.com
- DivorcedCatholic.com

- *Divorced. Catholic. Now What?*, Vince Frese and Lisa Duffy
- *The Catholic Guide to Dating After Divorce*, Lisa Duffy
- Recovering from Divorce Program, https://go.divorcedcatholic.com/getfree?utm_source=db

6. Discernment Help for Other Pathways
- vocation.com
- VianneyVocations.com

7. Helpful Inventories During Engagement
- Better Together – A Marriage Preparation Program, dynamiccatholic.com/marriage/better-together.html
- FOCCUS Pre-Marriage Inventory, foccusinc.com/foccus-inventory.aspx
- Focus on the Family: A Marriage Preparation Inventory v.3, https://media.focusonthefamily.com/boundless/pdf/marriage-inventory.pdf

ORGANIZATIONS AND APOSTOLATES

1. Homosexuality/Chastity Support
- Courage, couragerc.org
- Truth & Love, truthandlove.com
- Reintegrative Therapy Association, reintegrativetherapy.com
- Living Hope Ministries, livehope.org

2. **Contraceptives Alternatives**
   - You, Me, and NFP, YouMeandNFP.com
   - One More Soul, onemoresoul.com, 1-800-307-SOUL

3. **Pornography Recovery/Healing**
   - Covenant Eyes, covenanteyes.com, 1-877-479-1119
   - Family Life Center
   - Strive21, strive21.com
   - Restore Ministry, restoredministry.com/porn
   - True Knights, trueknights.org, 1-800-950-2008
   - Clean Heart, CleanHeart.online
   - Purity is Possible, purityispossible.com
   - Brain Heart World, www.brainheartworld.org
   - Fight the New Drug, www.fightthenewdrug.org/ overview

4. **Post-Abortion Healing**
   - Project Rachel, available in most cities
   - Rachel's Vineyard, www.rachelsvineyard.org

5. **Unplanned Pregnancy**
   - Bethany Christian Services, bethany.org/get-help/ pregnancy
   - 1-833-A-Good-Home or Text@8175000140
   - Legacy Adoption Services, legacyas.com/shes-pregnant

Appendix

Dating After Divorce by Vince Frese

1. After divorce, you are so vulnerable. You have just come out of such a destructive period of your life. All of your plans, hopes, and dreams are reduced to rubble. And, most likely, you have lived through a period where the one person you trusted the most to love you unconditionally has told you how unlovable you are. All of this creates a yearning—a yearning for that *true*, committed, life-giving love that now seems so elusive.

2. When we are vulnerable, we don't tend to make the best choices. We are acting out of pain and fear. This will drive you to jump into relationships before you are ready. Fortunately, we have a path to true love: our Catholic faith.

Here is the path to dating after divorce for a believer, and more particularly as a Catholic:

Before Dating

1. **Make Christ Your #1 Relationship.** Christ will never abandon you and he loves you unconditionally — for life. The primary ways to do this is through prayer and the Sacraments, especially the Eucharist.

2. **File for an Annulment**. Unless you receive an annulment, you are still bound to your marriage and are not free to date. The annulment process has the added benefit of helping you heal.

3. **Be Healed.** Just getting annulment doesn't mean you are ready to date. You need to be fully healed from your divorce before considering entering into new relationships. Be sure to take the time and seek out the people that can help you heal. Reach out to your parish and join a divorce support group. Seek out professional counseling. A good counselor can guide you through the healing process and let you know when you are ready to date.

When You Start to Date

Assuming you have an annulment, here is how to approach dating after divorce:

1. **Be All-In.** Commit to living your Catholic faith fully. The sooner you begin to adopt all of the life-giving teachings of our faith, the sooner you will develop a countenance that will be a magnet to other committed Catholics. So, ditch the cafeteria method of picking and choosing and be convicted of living *all* of your Catholic identity — even the hard stuff.

2. **Be the Person You Want to Meet.** If you want to meet a devout Catholic, then start with yourself. If you value traits such as honesty, authenticity, trustworthiness,

generosity, patience, and morality, then first develop those traits in yourself. Meeting a rock-solid Catholic starts by being one yourself!

3. **Be Transformed.** We become what we focus on. Making Christ the focus of your life by living your faith fully, going to Mass routinely, praying daily, and reading Scripture frequently, you will become more like him. It is then that you will naturally become irresistible to other people that are attracted to Christ.

4. **Commit to a Chaste Life.** Aside from being a serious sin, engaging in sex outside of marriage will never lead you to peace and will distort your decision-making. If the person you are dating truly has your best interests at heart, they will wait.

5. **Keep the Windshield Clear.** If you are driving down the road and your windshield is covered with mud, you are going to end up in a ditch. That's what happens to your life when you allow sin to build up. Sin blinds you to the guidance of the Holy Spirit. The key is to keep your windshield clear by going to confession on a routine basis. This will make sure you notice when Mr./Miss Right crosses your path.

6. **Forget Your Age.** Forget your age and remember this: virtue is ageless. A virtuous person is attractive no matter how old they are physically. Too many people focus

exclusively on their physical appearance. This naturally fades over time. Work on developing the habits that lead to an outstanding character and you will be irresistible to another rock-solid Catholic, no matter how old you are.

7. **Don't Settle.** Don't let your fear of being alone the rest of your life influence your decisions. If you do, you can end up being in a relationship with someone just because you feel like you are running out of time or options. Instead, trust that the Lord has an incredible plan for your life. By trusting, you are able to let go of the wheel and allow Him to guide you down the path to an abundant life of peace and joy. This trust will give you the courage to walk away from a relationship that is unhealthy or not part of God's amazing plan for your life.

Marriage Isn't for You[100]

What you're about to read is the real-life story of Seth Adam Smith in his own words. All I can tell you for now is that this changed my life forever. It will change your life forever as well. Do you know why? Because it relates to each one who reads it. Read till the end and you'll thank God for having read it.

Having been married only a year and a half, I've recently come to the conclusion that marriage isn't for me. Now before you start making assumptions, keep reading. I met my wife in

---

[100] Seth Adam Smith, "Marriage Isn't for You," November 2, 2013, http://sethadamsmith.com/2013/11/02/marriage-isnt-for-you.

high school when we were 15 years old. We were friends for ten years until…until we decided no longer wanted to be just friends. :) I strongly recommend that best friends fall in love. Good times will be had by all.

Nevertheless, falling in love with my best friend did not prevent me from having certain fears and anxieties about getting married. The nearer Kim and I approached the decision to marry, the more I was filled with a paralyzing fear. Was I ready? Was I making the right choice? Was Kim the right person to marry? Would she make me happy? Then, one fateful night, I shared these thoughts and concerns with my dad. Perhaps each of us have moments in our lives when it feels like time slows down or the air becomes still and everything around us seems to draw in, marking that moment as one we will never forget. My dad giving his response to my concerns was such a moment for me. With a knowing smile he said, "Seth, you're being totally selfish. So, I'm going to make this really simple: marriage isn't for you. You don't marry to make yourself happy, you marry to make someone else happy. More than that, your marriage isn't for yourself, you're marrying for a family. Not just for the in-laws and all of that nonsense, but for your future children. Who do you want to help you raise them? Who do you want to influence them?

Marriage isn't for you. It's not about you. Marriage is about the person you married." It was in that very moment that I knew that Kim was the right person to marry. I realized that I wanted to make her happy; to see her smile every day, to make her laugh every day. I wanted to be a part of her family, and my family wanted her to be a part of ours. And thinking back on all the times I had seen her play with my nieces, I knew that she was the one with whom I wanted to build our own family. My father's advice was both shocking and revelatory. It went against the grain of today's "Walmart philosophy", which is if it doesn't make you happy, you can take it back and get a new one. No, a true marriage (and true love) is never about you. It's about the person you love—their wants, their needs, their hopes, and their dreams. Selfishness demands, "What's in it for me?", while Love asks, "What can I give?"

Some time ago, my wife showed me what it means to love selflessly. For many months, my heart had been hardening with a mixture of fear and resentment. Then, after the pressure had built up to where neither of us could stand it, emotions erupted. I was callous. I was selfish. But instead of matching my selfishness, Kim did something beyond wonderful—she showed an outpouring of love. Laying aside all of the pain and anguish I had caused her, she lovingly took me in her arms and soothed my soul. I realized that I had forgotten my dad's advice. While Kim's side of the marriage had been to love me, my side of the marriage had become all about me. This awful realization brought me to tears, and I promised my wife that I would try to be better. To all who are reading this article— married, almost married, single, or even the sworn bachelor or bachelorette—I want you to know that marriage isn't for you. No true relationship of love is for you. Love is about the person you love. And, paradoxically, the more you truly love that person, the more love you receive. And not just from your significant other, but from their friends and their family and thousands of others you never would have met had your love remained self-centered. Truly, love and marriage isn't for you. It's for others. A lot of marriages could be saved if you share this story with others.

Karol Wojtyla, athlete, poet, actor, priest, Pope, Saint (John Paul II)

"The person who does not decide to love forever will find it very hard really to love even for one day."

Made in the USA
Las Vegas, NV
20 May 2023

72321284R10095